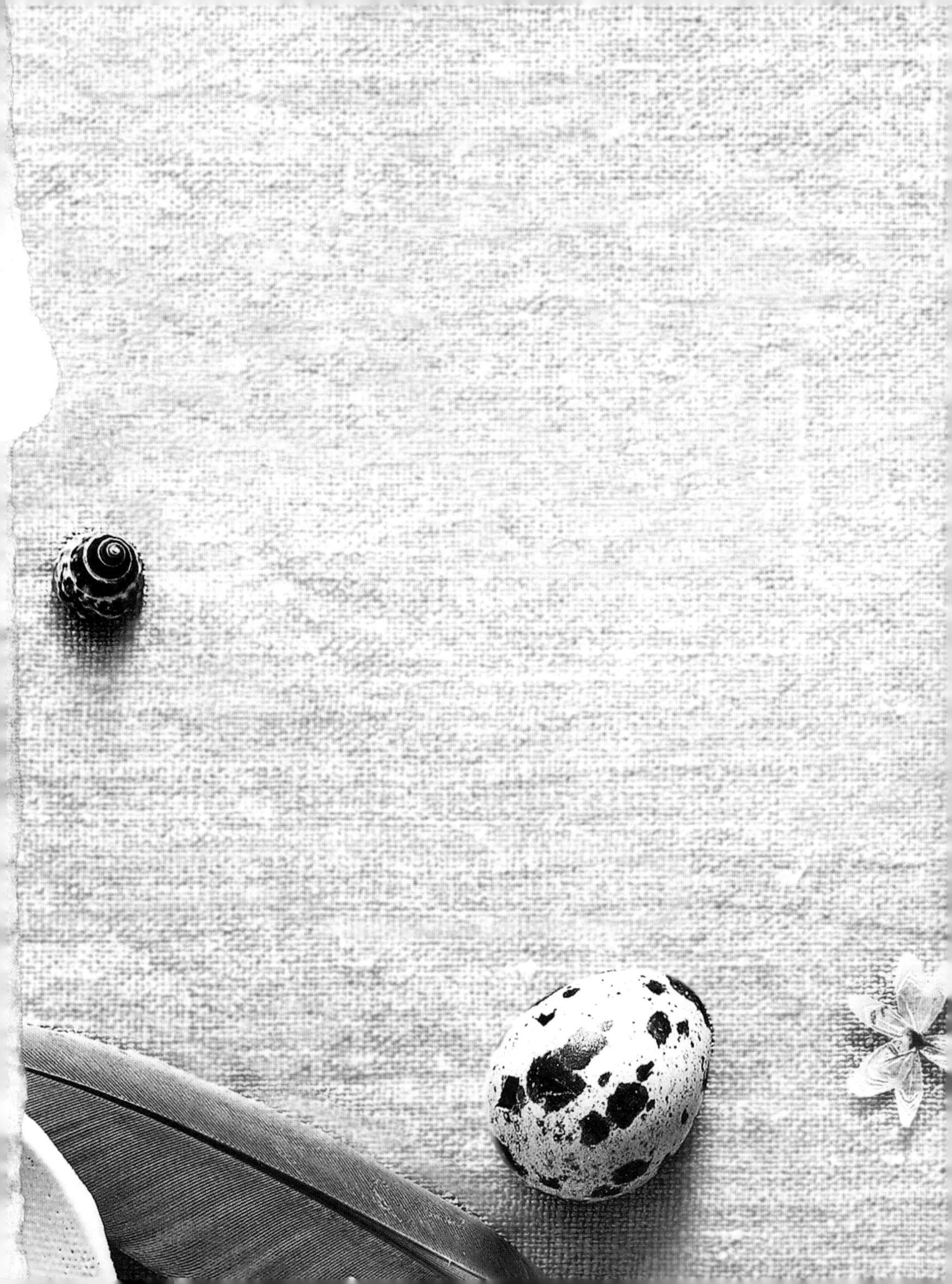

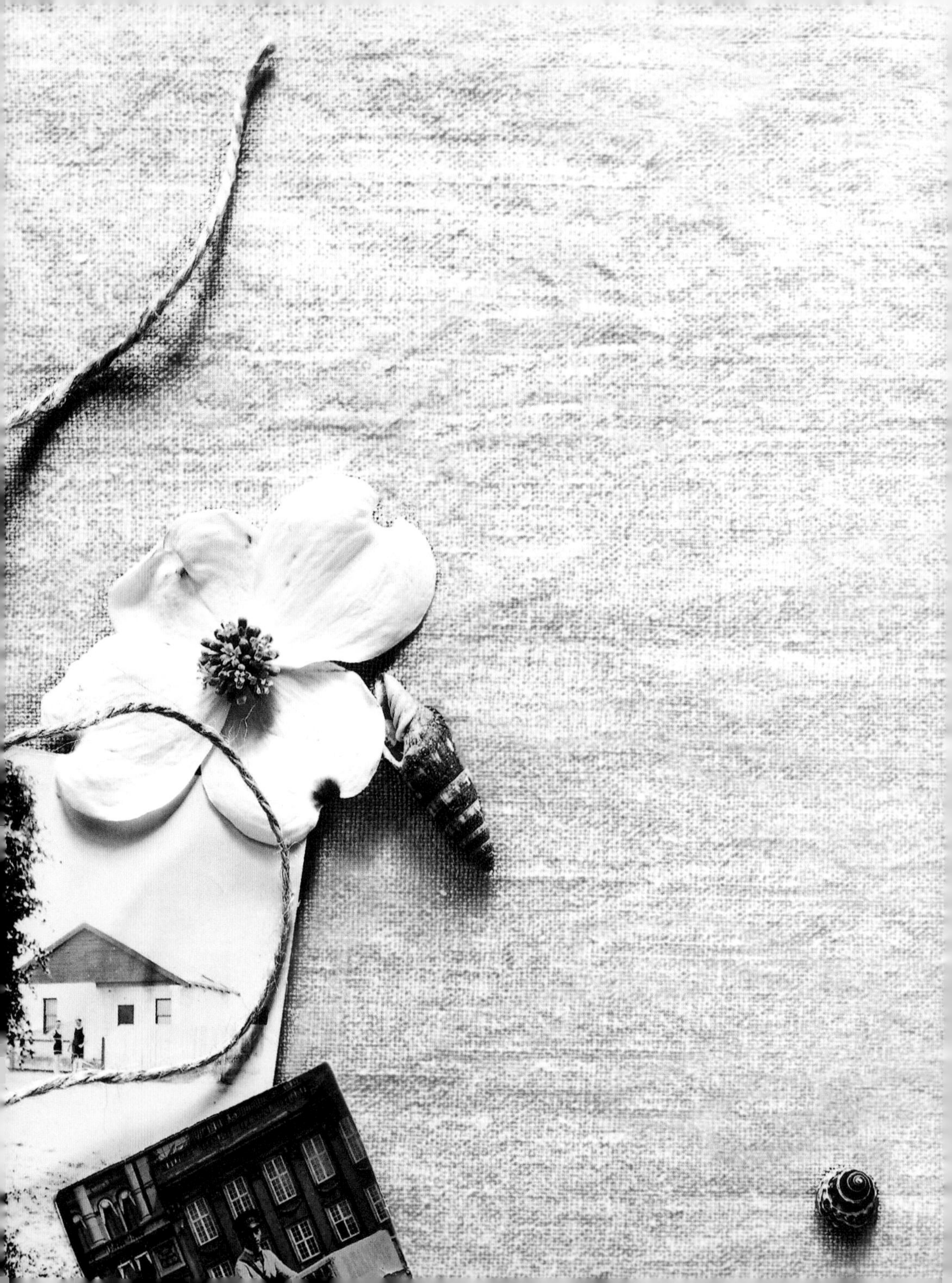

Plan B.

A guide to navigating and embracing change

Shannah Kennedy

For Mum.
My friend and my teacher.
Your incredible strength, ability to adapt and
positive mindset have taught me so much.
You have been the inspiration for this book.

THE JOURNEY

STAGE 1
RECOGNISE &
RESPOND
The Change

STAGE 2
RESTORE &
RECOVER
The Healing

Stop. Breathe.
Start where you are
Express the event
Feel the pain and name it
Understand your emotions

Acknowledge your feelings and fear
Develop an immediate survival plan
Understand your feelings
Assess and take stock
Dance with fear

Embrace the grief
Understand the stages of grief
Practise radical self-compassion
Choose your path with care

Choose your narrative
What's your story?
Deal with others
Stay connected
This too shall pass

Sink into self-care
Bathe in extreme self-care
Master your calm with self-connection and breath
Move through overwhelm with FLOW and RAIN

Renew and refuel
Restore your four pillars of health
Establish supportive routines and rituals
Heal through mindfulness

Open the path to positivity
Practise loving-kindness (metta)
Give yourself permission to let go
Start saying yes!
Flow and identify the gift

Relinquish the past – you've got this
Feel the small wins
Find patience and hope
Set small timelines

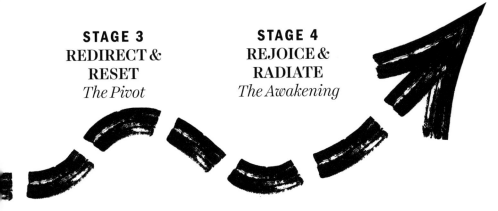

STAGE 3
REDIRECT &
RESET
The Pivot

STAGE 4
REJOICE &
RADIATE
The Awakening

Rebuild your foundation
Redefine your values and purpose
Clarify what you want
Upgrade your attitude

Plant new seeds
Challenge your comfort zone
Train your brain
Set boundaries

Create your road map
Simplify your life
Write your new vision
Set fresh goals

Ignite your flame
Choose your cheer squad
Practise visualisation
Be the change you wish to see

Embark on the journey
Manage your time and expectations
Conquer limiting beliefs
Power up your happy habits

Embrace joy
Fire up your creativity
Plan your celebrations
Random acts of kindness

Claim your personal power
Fostering resilience and hardiness
Create your power questions
Create space for reflection

Celebrate the awakening
Experience a grateful life
Be the light
Write a letter to your future self

A NOTE FROM SHANNAH

Change can turn our plans, our lives and our dreams upside down. Whether you have faced a redundancy, had a relationship breakdown, lost a loved one, been in an accident, had a health scare, or been affected by an economic downturn, your ability to accept, adapt and build a new plan will be the key to your future happiness.

I have been a coach and strategist for twenty years and have had the pleasure and privilege of working with clients around the world as they've dealt with change at work, with health, with intimate relationships or with family dynamics. I have guided people as they have found themselves in a great storm and I have helped them to find calm waters once again. I have also been in the eye of that storm myself.

I know that the ability to adapt to a crisis – or an opportunity – is the key to happiness and inner harmony, and to finding our fulfilment, joy and success once again.

Pivoting to Plan B allows us to change direction. It allows us to reset and move forward in life.

A pivot in personal life is a fundamental change in our life strategy.

In 2015 I wrote *The Life Plan* to help people around the world live bigger, better, whole and more meaningful lives. Now I want to help you adapt that plan. Having a Plan B has always been a part of my philosophy and there has never been a time when it has been more necessary.

I have written this book to simplify the incredibly complicated journey we go on when we experience a change in life. I trust it will guide you towards unlearning the old ways, old thoughts and old dreams, and show you how to grow, adapt and create a new plan. As you reclaim your personal power and create a new mindset, you will embrace a new and wiser version of yourself. You will learn to get up each day and put one foot in front of the other and create a new energy, a new level of self-care, a new routine and a new life. When you feel in the depths of despair, this book will be your pathway to grieving, healing and building a new, bigger and more empowered life for yourself. It will be your reassurance that Plan B can be as good as Plan A, or better, or just different.

This book is written from my heart. It is for all those people I know and have worked with over the past twenty years who would have loved to have this book next to them as a roadmap to finding happiness once again.

This book is a guide for you.

This book is your retreat.

This book is for you to reclaim your power.

This book is for you to rebuild yourself and reconnect with yourself.

This book is for you to use to get to the other side.

This book is a simple guide to move through change.

This book is your lighthouse in the storm.

My gift to you,

Shannah x

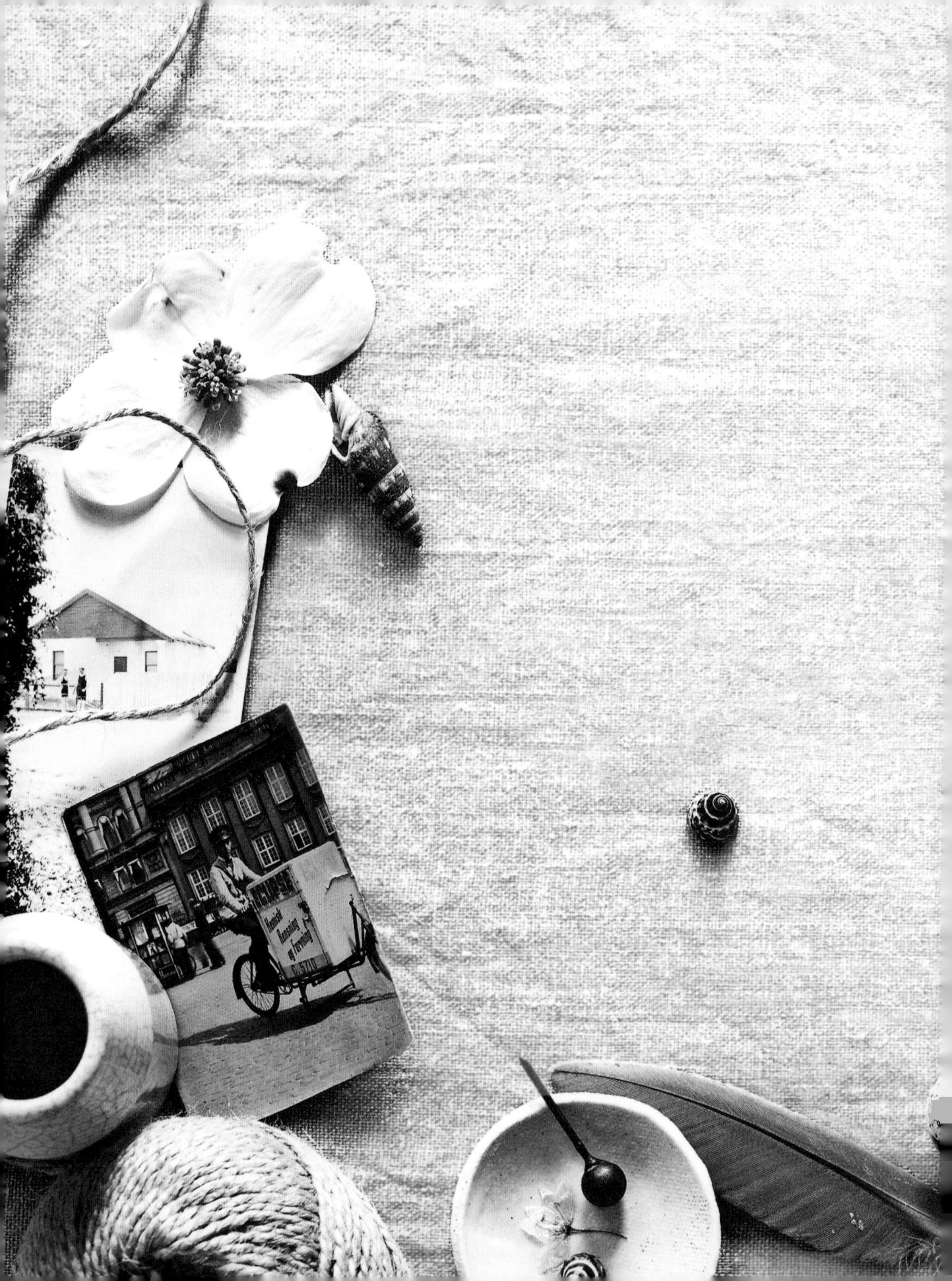
Kemisk
Rensning
og Farvning
C 5710

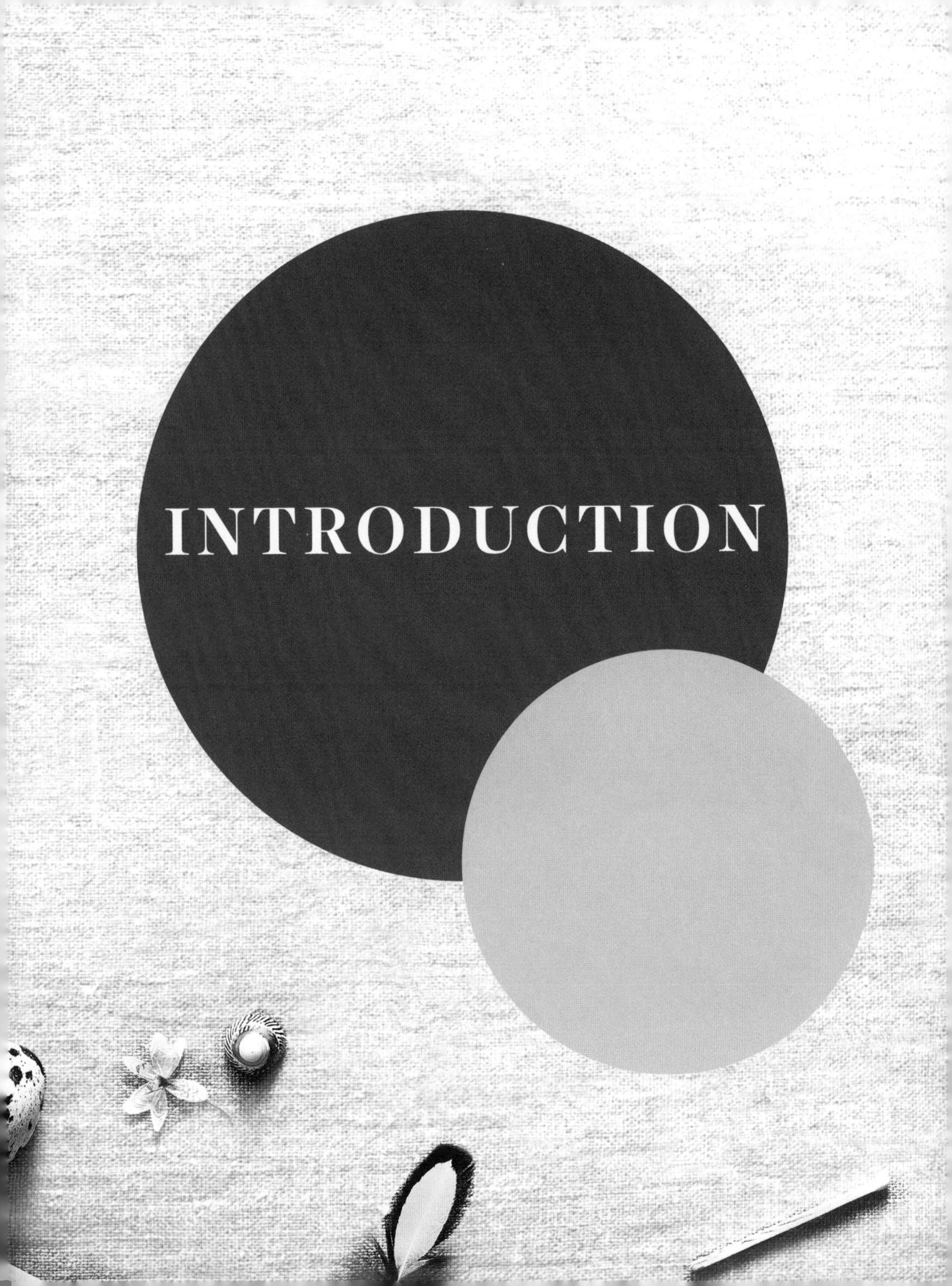

INTRODUCTION

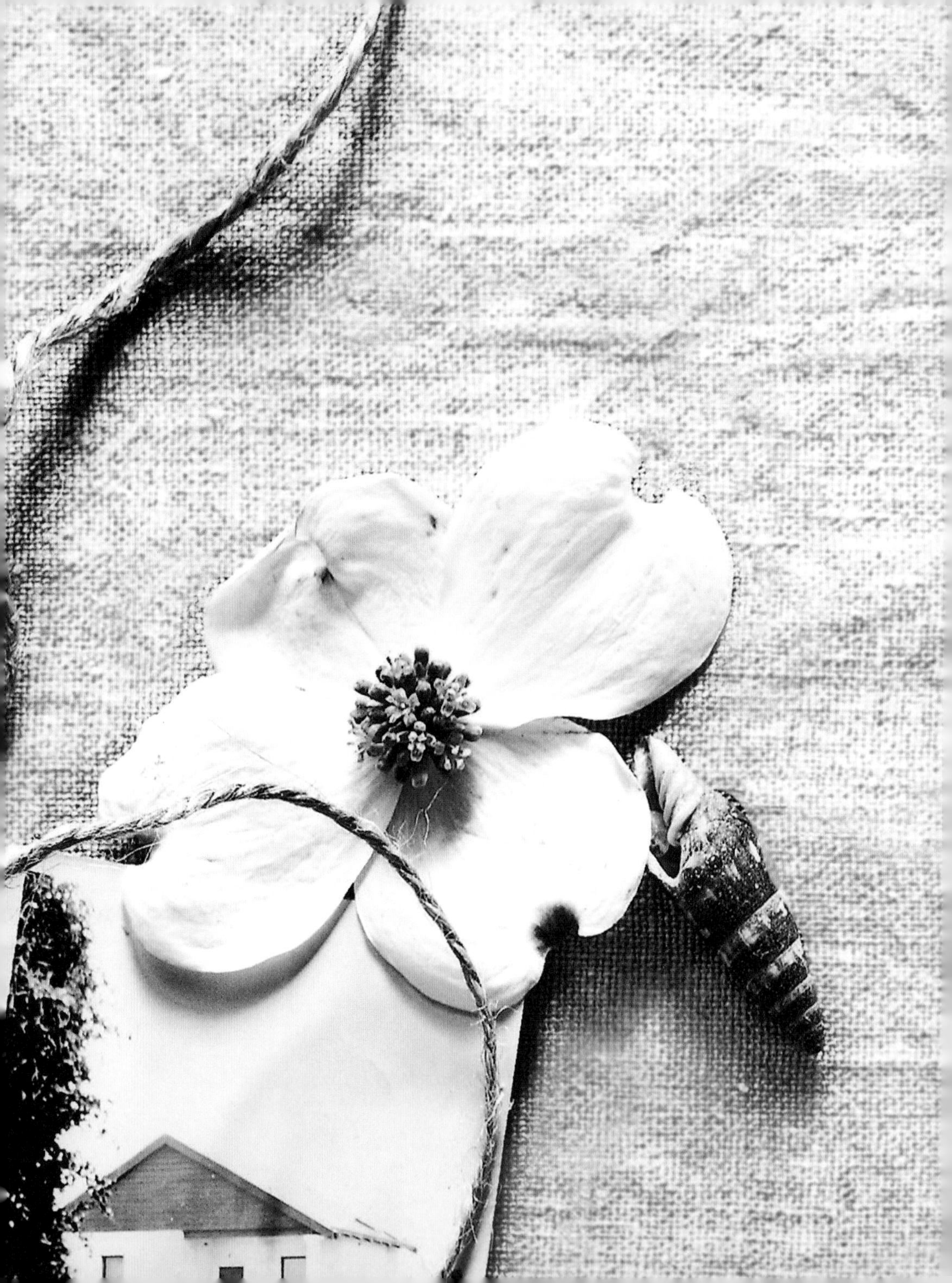

Challenges are gifts that force us to search for a new centre of gravity. Don't fight them. Just find a new way to stand.

_____

Oprah Winfrey

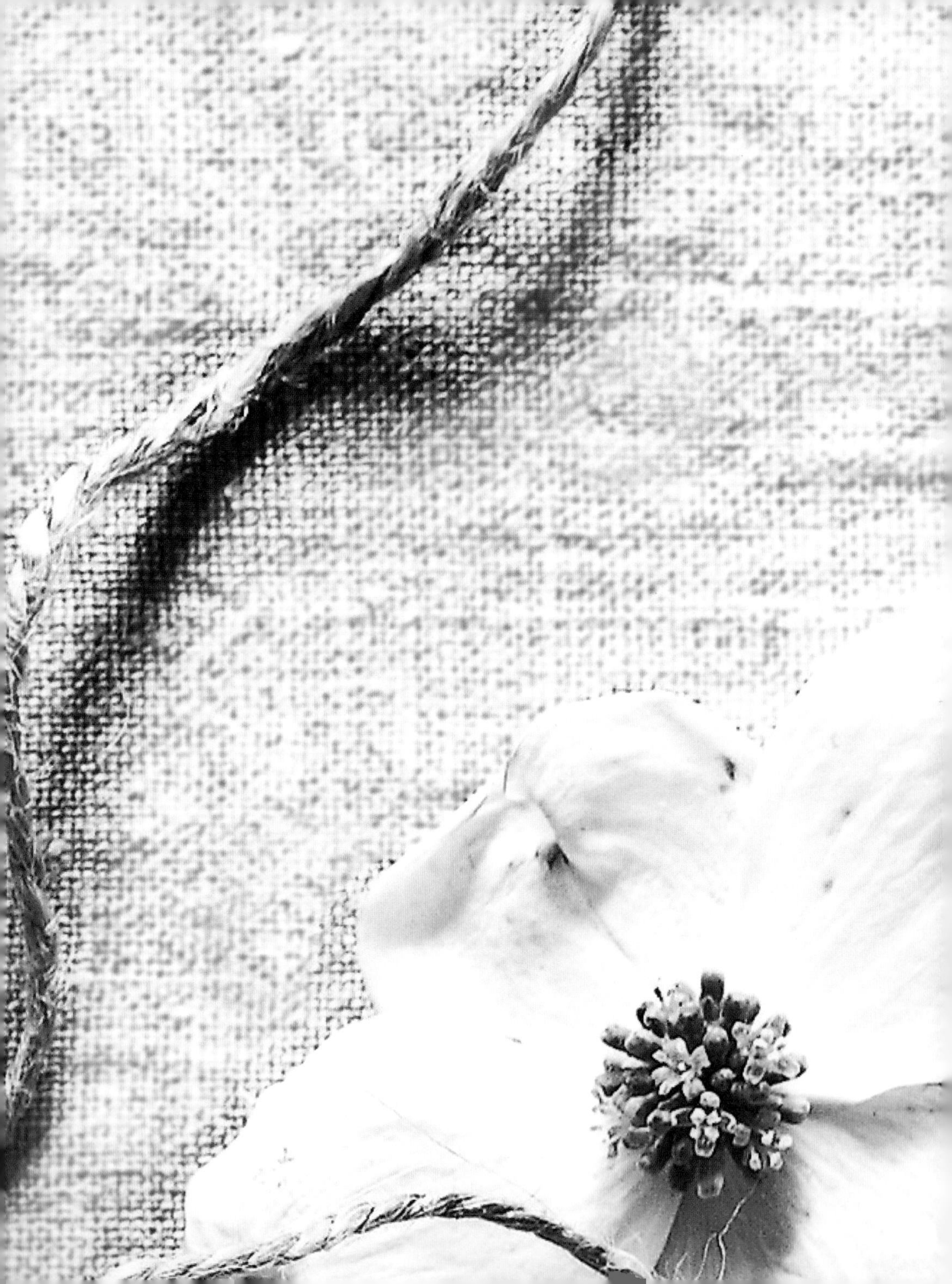

MY
STORY

For eight years I worked in sports management, sponsorship and PR. In 1999 I was at what I thought was the peak of my success – I had A-class tickets to events, money and a glamorous lifestyle mixing with our country's superstars. I would burn the candle at both ends, living on adrenaline. It was exciting, intoxicating, thrilling and fast. As a Type A overachieving perfectionist, I did not rest, I could not sit still, and when I had time off I filled it with going out, exercising and avoiding being by myself or allowing myself to experience deep feelings in a relationship.

Then one day it all came crashing down. My body could no longer keep up that relentless pace, complete the never-ending goal sheet I kept creating for myself or serve my addiction to avoiding being still with myself.

I lost my health. My mind stopped. My body stopped. My life stopped. I felt paralysed. I could not move, could not think, could not function, and I experienced pain like I had never felt before. Chronic fatigue syndrome broke my mind and body, and it came calling with its best friend: depression.

I could not do anything, create anything or work for a year. Grounded and unable to function, I experienced a huge range of emotions – shock, confusion, blame, frustration, shame, embarrassment, anxiety, anger, overwhelm, helplessness, loneliness, pain, loss, grief. The question came into my mind and body, 'Who am I without my job?'

I had loved my title and the security it gave me. My job defined me. It defined the athletes I worked with, too. They had deep confidence that stemmed from their job title, the car they drove, the travel, the applause, the medals, the accolades and the fans. I had seen the great loss in many of them when their sporting career was suddenly over – through injury, being dropped from the team, early forced retirement, their body breaking down, their club folding, a media scandal. An athlete can lose their career at any time.

I had noticed that athletes who had not done any inner work – built themselves as a person first – and instead defined themselves by their career, marriage, title and status, fell the hardest when a curve ball was thrown. Because their confidence had been built from external factors, not from within, once they no longer had the title that defined them they felt lost. It was, in reality, a false confidence.

I had not done any inner work either, and I came to the realisation that I was externally driven. My reliance on success was not based on knowing, loving, caring and connecting with my true self.

My ill health was my moment in life to change. It forced me to reassess and throw my plans in the bin. I had to start again.

Slowly over the following year, with help, guidance and support, I built a new plan – Plan B – which involved developing a body, mind and soul that were deeply connected to self: sustainable and healthy, with an empowered mindset, with new control and a calm confidence. I experienced every emotion, learnt about it and wrote about it. Over time I built a new and better version of myself, a new life for myself and a new future for myself. My emotions gradually moved to empowerment, security, meaning, self-esteem, joy, love, confidence and connection, abundance and inner harmony.

I decided to employ a life coach and to study life coaching, though back then it was a term few people had heard of. Then, with my diploma and drawing upon my own journey, I became a life coach to athletes, to coach them into retirement. I became passionate about building the person, so they could transition with confidence, direction, clarity and new purpose. I helped them through the stages of grief in order to come to terms with the loss of their sporting family and taught them to understand that life off the field can be as exciting, rewarding and fulfilling as life on the field. I also worked with those who had just hit the big time and developed a safety net for them, a Plan B running alongside their career plan.

The athletes I worked with came to the realisation that their job was what they did but it did not solely define them as a person. As we created a life outside of their role, we built the whole person, which gave them deep inner confidence. They were possibly studying for their future career, learning about leadership, developing a network outside of sport, diving deeply into their values and investing in self-care, self-management and self-leadership skills and had projects ready to go for rainy days or when the unexpected happened.

I knew I had found my calling, but I also knew that this work wasn't just important for athletes. We all need to take control of ourselves, understand ourselves, love ourselves and define who we are as a person, and redefine it again as life changes. We all need to connect with our true power, our wholehearted self, to be empowered, feel inner harmony, calm confidence and stay grounded when in a crisis situation.

I broadened my client list and began working with highly successful business owners and CEOs who, when faced with retirement or a new role, can experience overwhelming emotions of loss, loneliness, anxiety and self-doubt. Some I helped had never experienced such emotional turmoil as losing their title and the perceived status that came with it. Their journey, their transition through change to rediscovering who they were without the brand, business or title behind them was incredible. They began to bloom and flourish in their own right.

I also helped people through relationship breakdowns, affairs, loss of a loved one, major changes in health, and friendships ending. I saw my role – and still do – as bridging the gap from where the client is now to where they want to be in the future. The journey will most often mean rebuilding their thoughts, emotions, habits, plans and future visions. Softening the fear, learning to forgive and letting go of resentment are necessary so they can live freely again.

It has been a privilege to witness their incredible growth, to believe in them, to be their cheerleader, their coach and their lighthouse as they have reclaimed themselves, and to support them as their dreams have come true.

The world has had no greater need to adapt, change and create a new plan than during 2020's COVID-19 pandemic. We were all thrown in the deep end and it has put us to the test. Many of us have gone through a range of emotions, including fear, grief, loss, anxiety, overwhelm and anger.

During lockdown my business, like many others, came to a halt. All speaking bookings for the year were cancelled. All of my work and main income for the year diasappeared within that first week of lockdown. But having already changed my life and adapted to change in the past, I felt calm, accepting, even a little excited by the prospect. Why excited? Because I knew I had done the work on myself. Living with chronic fatigue syndrome and depression means that I am constantly having to assess my thoughts, diet, sleep, exercise and supplement intake. My body and mind just will not keep up with my

Life Plan A, so I always have a Plan B and a Plan C. I saw lockdown as an opportunity. The opportunity to be at home as a family; the opportunity to clean out my home, my business, my life, to reset again. The emotions would flood in during the day, just as they did for everyone else – what if I have to start my business all over again, what if no one wants coaching ever again, what if, what if, what if – but I knew I'd been here before. My calm returned quickly and I noticed that I was able to lean in, to avoid distracting myself, to sit still and experience being highly uncomfortable and to experience and process emotions quickly.

My hope now is to instil this confidence in you and guide you through the change process.

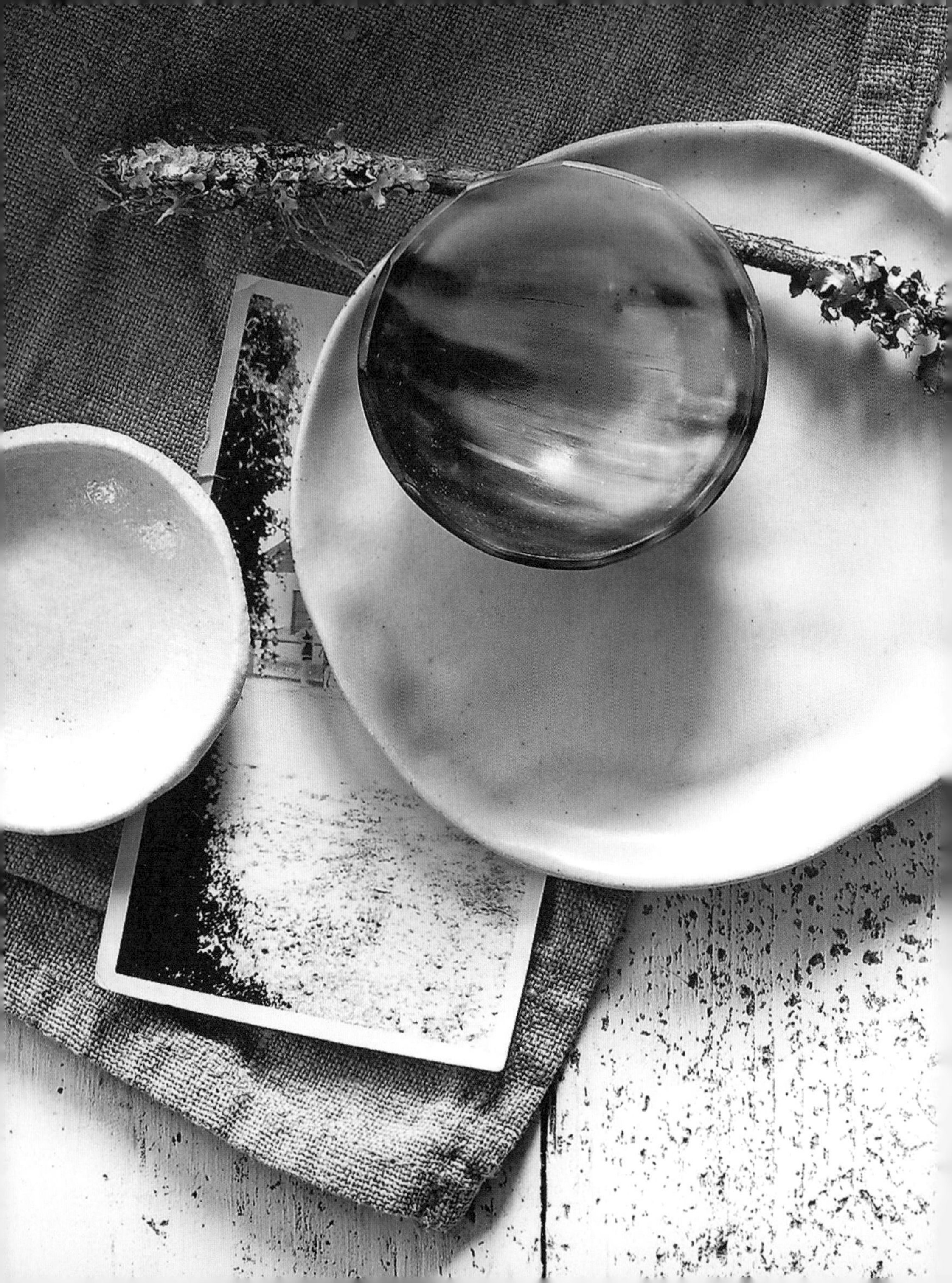

RECOGNISE & RESPOND

Stage 1

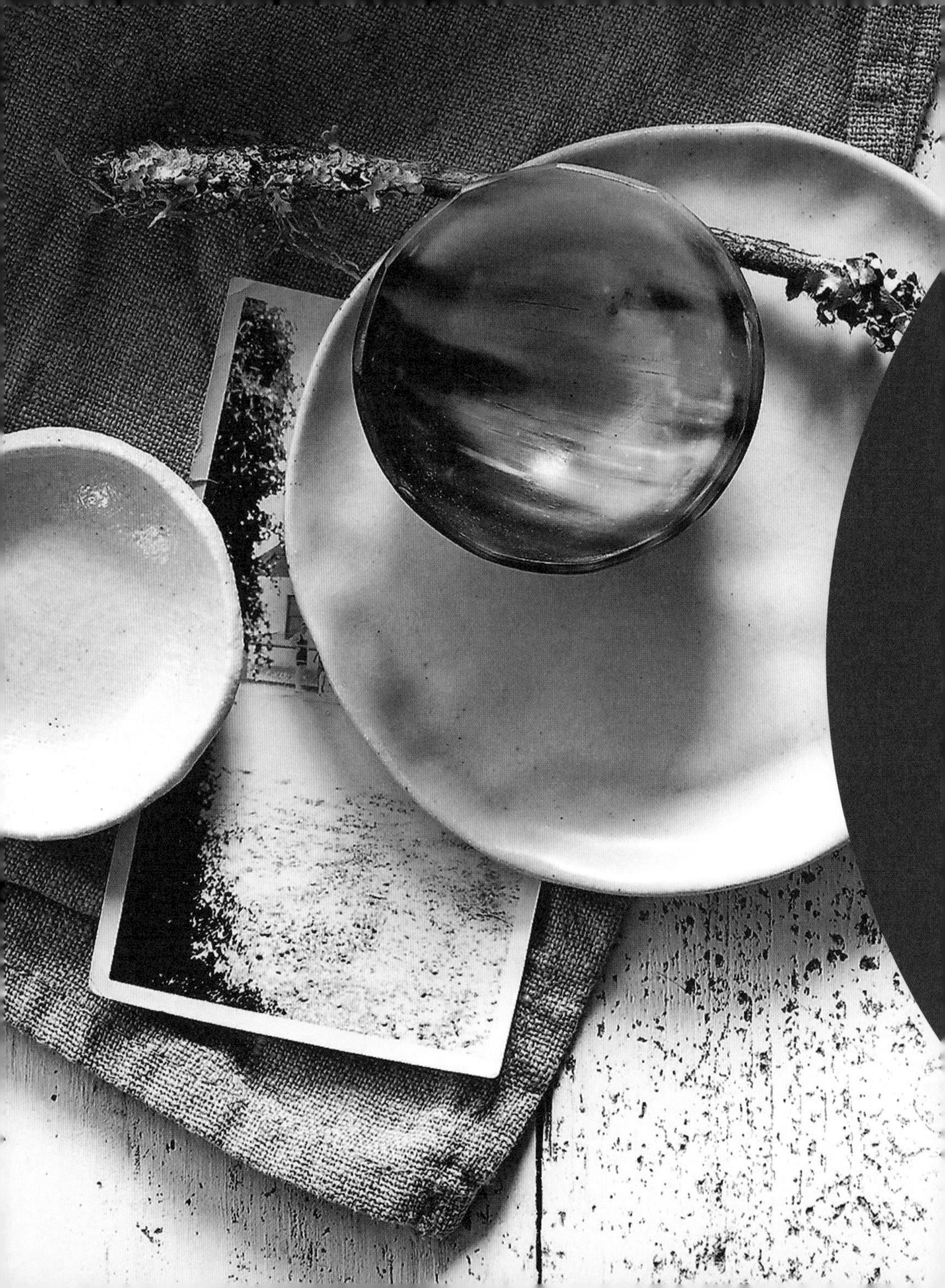

Stage 1

RECOGNISE & RESPOND

THE CHANGE

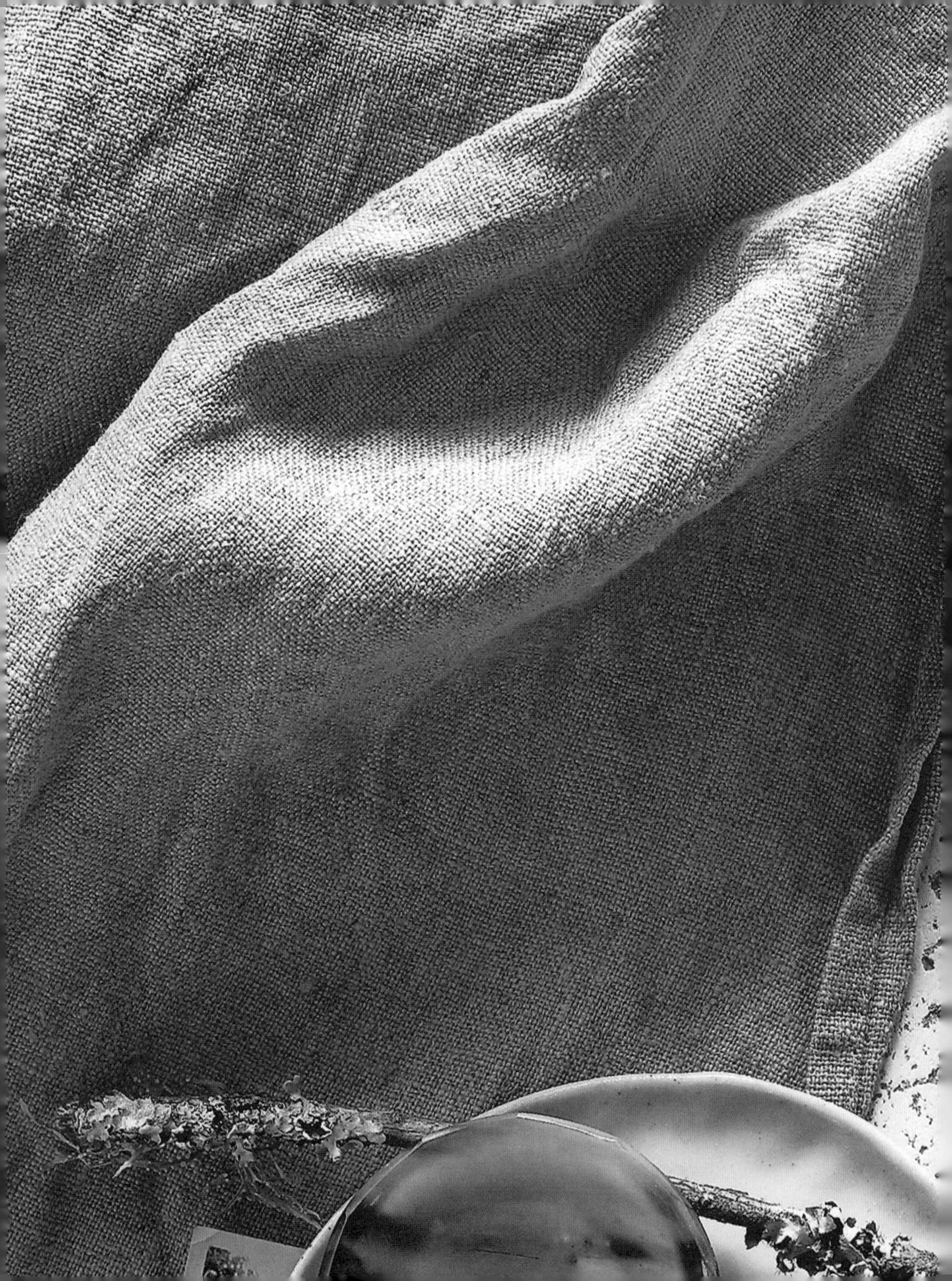

Change is hardest in the beginning, messy in the middle and best at the end.

Robin Sharma

Life is in constant transition. The world changes every day, every hour, every minute. Change is inevitable. It can be positive and exhilarating and take us to a whole new level, full of excitement, awe and overwhelming joy, but it can also be devastating and throw us into the depths of loneliness, pain and despair.

Change may be something you saw coming and thought was inevitable, but more often than not it blindsides you. Regardless of whether you anticipated the change, the first stage you must go through in order to pivot is to recognise and respond to the situation you are in. This is how you will survive and start to move forward. This is the beginning of finding your calm and establishing some emotional balance.

You will need to begin to process the loss of what was, of life before the change, by creating a plan for yourself to move towards the positive. Acknowledge that you are now in the business of coping, changing and conquering.

It is a time to be gentle with yourself. Acknowledge your unique constitution and work within your limitations, as some of us are hardier than others and we all grow at different rates.

Then, I invite you to review, reset and refocus. Imagine I am sitting with you and I ask you to begin writing a new chapter in your life. Acknowledge that the last chapter didn't necessarily end well, but we have turned the page and can now work on a new story. What comes next for you? Let's write the story. Reveal how you are going to deal with the situation, the people, the broken pieces. I invite you to dig deep to find the gifts the universe has in store for you.

4. Choose your narrative

What's your story?

Dealing with others

Stay connected

This too shall pass

2. Acknowledge your feelings and fear

Develop an immediate survival plan

Understand your feelings

Assess and take stock

Dance with fear

3. Embrace the grief

Understand the stages of grief

Practise radical self-compassion

Choose your path with care

1. Stop. Breathe.

Start where you are

Express the event

Feel the pain and name it

Understand your emotions

The truest, most beautiful life never promises to be an easy one. We need to let go of the lie that it's supposed to be.

Glennon Doyle

Untamed

At the end of my career in sports management and sponsorship I knew my life had to change. Not only did I have chronic fatigue syndrome, I also didn't agree with the direction the company was going in. It had been bought by a larger company and no longer had a family feel. The culture of care I had loved was being destroyed and it seemed to me that profit was now king.

The day I resigned I was terrified. My heart was racing, my knees were shaking and I felt sick in my stomach. Was I making the right choice? What if I got it wrong? What if I failed? What if I got it right? I didn't have any answers, but my intuition said, 'Do it – follow your instinct.'

I never expected the tidal waves of emotion that flooded through me, considering I was the one driving the change. The fear of failure, the sadness of leaving a job I felt married to, the excitement at what the universe might deliver to me, the realisation that I had no idea who I was without my job. My life had been consumed by work, and I had surrounded myself with my colleagues and team of athletes.

As soon as I was on my own, I felt an incredible emptiness, a loneliness. The shallowness of my life hit me, and now that I no longer had a company car, credit card or phone, I felt stripped of choices and security.

I had to make a plan, to create a script of what I could say when people asked, 'Why the hell would you leave your great job and become a life coach?' There were so few life coaches then that not many people knew about them. I had to deal with other people's negativity, as well as my own grief that my body was changing the course of my life, and I had to create a life more in step with my health challenges.

In truth, the best journey of my life started that day. It was the journey to accept, embrace and focus on what I could control. Chronic fatigue syndrome and I are now partners in crime. I have had to learn to dance with it, respect it, nurture it and listen to it.

Stop. Breathe.

Your life just changed. Your world has gone into a spin, and you feel like you are out of control. As your mind races, you feel fear and experience shock, denial and numbness all at the same time. What just happened? As your mind races, your body shakes. In that moment you need to stop and breathe. Stop what you are doing, stop your routine, stop your to-do list, stop the expectations you have of yourself and others and ground yourself in breath.

Air is the first food of the newborn – **Edward Rosenfeld**

Breathing is the first energy input, it is the prana, the life force.

This is survival. Life as you knew it just changed, so give yourself permission to allow the air in, to create space for yourself internally, to draw a line in the sand and to stop the onslaught of thoughts pouring in so fast that your head feels like it will explode. Give yourself a moment to stop, slow down and take a breath. That's all you need to do right now. Try deep abdominal breathing to trigger the relaxation response. Give yourself permission. Breathe.

Breathing Ritual 1

Breathe in: 'I am breathing in'

Breathe out: 'I am letting go'

Breathing Ritual 2

Breathe in: 'I am here'

Breathe out: 'I am present, I am safe'

Start where you are, use what you have, do what you can.

Arthur Ashe

START WHERE YOU ARE

You had a plan, you had a vision for your life, you thought you were in total control, but life had other ideas. We often think we know how we might react in certain situations, but when the time comes we are unable to anticipate the incredible wave of physical and emotional feelings that fully engulf us even if we have planned for that situation.

In times of stress, either good stress or bad, your body releases adrenaline, your heart beats faster and your blood pressure changes. A cascade of stress hormones is released around the body. You know what it feels like. Your body changes state. Your breath becomes shallow and rapid, your mouth might get dry and your hands can become sweaty. These are natural reactions and part of the fight-or-flight response which allows you to react to perceived sudden danger. Some people can regain control quickly; for others it may bring on a panic attack, which will lead to anxiety and an overload of stressful thoughts and feelings. In the latter situation, the ability to regain some control can be a lengthy process.

I recall many stressful moments in my life. Breaking up with my first boyfriend after we'd been together for five years. Being overseas at age twenty-one and locked in a room with my boss, feeling sheer terror as he gave me an ultimatum to sleep with him if I wanted to keep my job. (I declined and he made my life utterly miserable at work.) Being harassed constantly at work in the early 1990s for being a woman in a male-dominated profession. Getting phone calls from my mum when young relatives died. Friends and colleagues taking their lives. Family conflict. There were many moments like these that took my breath away. They hurt me; they changed me.

Perhaps the biggest change was, of course, burning out before the age of thirty and being diagnosed with chronic fatigue syndrome (CFS). When loneliness and depression came calling I found myself rocking in the corner of a room, not understanding how this could have happened when I had a good life. Deep down I knew that I could not keep up with other people anymore: that I needed rest, real rest.

The day I had to surrender to CFS was the saddest, most confronting day of my life. I could no longer lift my head off the pillow. I was so angry at my body for not being able to keep up with my mind. I knew I had to change my plans: the way I thought, the way I lived, the way I worked, the way I viewed success. Life had thrown me a curve ball, a long, slow, breaking pitch, just like a baseballer trying to keep a hitter off balance. I was definitely off balance. I was incredibly stressed: mentally, physically, emotionally and spiritually. I felt completely broken, and when depression moved in it just added to the wreckage. There was no quick fix. There was no solution. No magic pill. I felt deep, deep sadness.

All I could do was breathe.

EXPRESS THE EVENT

Writing can help you organise your thoughts and start the process of regulating your emotions. It can help you break free from the endless mental chatter and the cycle you may be stuck in. It can help you connect with your inner feelings and desires as well as reduce stress symptoms and boost mood.

Writing has been my medicine. I write out my anger, frustration and resentment when waves of CFS, depression or external events rock me. I know I need to dance with my health challenges and structure my life to accommodate them, but I do not let them rule me. Rather than speaking about it so much now, I have learnt the power of the written word.

The more I write, the more it flows out of me, the less overwhelmed I feel.

When you are ready, and only when you are ready and you can breathe again, take a quick look at what just happened, express it, write it down, and get it out of your mind. I invite you now to write down here exactly what happened. Where you were, who you were with, what day it was, what the weather was like. With all of my clients, I invite them to write daily, to journal, to express the overwhelm and give those negative thoughts and fears a place to go – out through the pen and onto the page instead of bottling everything up. This is the most powerful start you can give yourself. So write down what happened with no judgement, but rather with kindness and compassion for yourself.

It may be that you are unable to tell friends and family about what you are experiencing. In that case, I would invite you to write to them. I did the same in October 2019, when I was suffering a relapse and could not speak. I wanted to share with my friends what I was going through, but I was unable to do it in person.

Here's what I wrote.

I have not spoken about my struggles before with many people, other than surface level. I have had chronic fatigue for twenty years. I have had depression for twenty years and have managed it well and kept it inside. Life coaches have to have their shit together! I got myself onto a natural rather than synthetic antidepressant which I was really proud of (silly, I know). I was doing well, always had some bad and depressive thoughts and self-loathing and imposter syndrome thoughts going on, but always in control of them and could sit with it and then 'coach' myself out of it. When the medication ran out, and the supplier stopped manufacturing it, I thought, 'Oh well, I will be all right!' I had a very slippery and steady four-week decline, my thoughts spiralling – my rational thinking and reasoning went out the window. I blamed the moon, the weather. The phone wasn't ringing with new clients, so I thought I was a crap coach and I should just shut up shop. The inner self-critic was out to get me.

I cannot cook, I cannot do . . . Until the day that I just couldn't move, foetal position, crying uncontrollably, and thinking life would be better if I was not here. The only thing I could do was tell myself to breathe. This ended in a horrendous migraine and I felt like a 1000 kg weight fell on my head and heart.

I did put my hand up. I rang a friend who said to go straight to the doctor. So I did. I don't know how I got there. I sat in her rooms bawling my eyes out and couldn't explain why. She said she was going to be the boss now and take care of me. I had to listen to her. I had to put my own pride away. Now, ten days later, the fog is lifting, the antidepressants are kicking in, the headache is subsiding and I am exhausted, but there is a glimpse of my old self back. I have to get my head around being okay with taking the pills, that I am not defeated but rather supporting myself.

I am fabulous at giving but not great at receiving. I have never been able to receive well and it is a new skill I need to learn. My husband and kids have been outstanding. So compassionate and kind. Thank you for being there when I was so incredibly vulnerable and scared.

I have to manage the dark clouds and I realise that I cannot do this alone. Thank you for your non-judgemental, supportive and inspirational friendship.

Look forward to a cup of tea soon.

FEEL THE PAIN
AND NAME IT

What pain do you feel? Can you name it? I have these incredible conversations with my clients where I ask them to actually name the exact pain they are feeling. This is a chance to stop and specify the pain. Do you feel it in your throat? Your gut? Your chest? I know that when you sit in the pain, feel it, be still with it, and name it, it has a chance to move through you. The fact that you acknowledge it, hear it and feel it will allow it to start moving away. Writing about your life event or trauma and naming the pain or overwhelm allows you to process the experience in a safe place, which is the start of the journey towards healing and growth. Right now, right where you are, write down everything you are feeling, experiencing, thinking.

Sit with the pain until the wave passes, then feel the calm. Know you can ride these waves and let them go.

Allowing yourself to sit in the pain, feel it and name it, resisting the urge to get rid of it, and then releasing it allows the new flow to happen. Although painful, it is the start of the healing journey. I did this recently when I learnt that my cousin's beautiful wife had had a heart attack and passed away aged fifty-eight. She was happy, put family first, kept life simple and had a great work ethic. A pure and happy soul. I sat there in the news, the pain, the memories of her, and I felt my stomach ache. My bones felt like lead and my eyes burned as they tried to see the memories. I allowed myself to sit perfectly still, to feel it, to honour her, to not avoid it and distract myself. Where do you feel the pain?

UNDERSTAND YOUR EMOTIONS

There is a high cost to avoiding our emotions and feelings: increased stress, confusion and sabotaging our wellbeing. Emotions are chemical reactions that are released in our bodies, not just our minds, in response to a trigger or event. They form a feedback loop between our physical bodies and our minds.

Don't swim against your emotions. You can sit with them. You do not need to battle your emotions and fight the way you feel.

Emotions are the fuel for our feelings. They are a natural part of our lives. Their purpose is to let us know how we are being affected by the things that are going on in our lives. They are the signal to help us identify and make sense of what is happening and what we are going through. And while these feelings may be scary and uncomfortable at times, by making an effort to learn to understand them, flow with them and work with them, we can better understand ourselves and uncover our underlying needs, wants and beliefs.

The first step to dealing with emotions effectively is to identify them, name and label them.

Finding the right words will allow you to see the real issue, to take the messy experience you have on your hands, understand it and build a roadmap for moving forward. Sitting with emotions can lighten the weight of shame, soften our fear, and guide us back to our source of wisdom. We can learn to make peace with our emotions as we ride the waves of change. Don't suppress the feelings – express them right here.

On the next page there is a list of emotions, by Dr Susan David. Write out below the emotions you are currently feeling.

A LIST OF EMOTIONS

Go beyond the obvious to identify exactly what you're feeling.

ANGRY	SAD	ANXIOUS
Grumpy	Disappointed	Afraid
Frustrated	Mournful	Stressed
Annoyed	Regretful	Vulnerable
Defensive	Depressed	Confused
Spiteful	Paralysed	Bewildered
Impatient	Pessimistic	Sceptical
Disgusted	Tearful	Worried
Offended	Dismayed	Cautious
Irritated	Disillusioned	Nervous

HURT	EMBARRASSED	HAPPY
Jealous	Isolated	Thankful
Betrayed	Self-conscious	Trusting
Isolated	Lonely	Comfortable
Shocked	Inferior	Content
Deprived	Guilty	Excited
Victimised	Ashamed	Relaxed
Aggrieved	Repugnant	Relieved
Tormented	Pathetic	Elated
Abandoned	Confused	Confident

Source: Dr Susan David

MY CURRENT EMOTIONS ARE:

DISCOVER HOW TO SOFTEN YOUR EMOTIONS BY STAYING WITH THEM

'I feel so hurt that my partner has left me. I am so worried about what this means for my future. I feel like I want to cry, my throat is closing, I feel so vulnerable, so uncomfortable in this feeling, but I am okay, I can move through this.'

VALIDATE YOUR EMOTIONS, ACCEPTING THEM WITHOUT JUDGEMENT

'I feel so angry at the moment, so hurt, so embarrassed. So lost.'

FOCUS ON THE PRESENT SO YOU DON'T WALLOW IN OR GET FIXATED ON YOUR EMOTIONS

'This feels so awful! But I am just driving home right now, and that is what I need to bring my attention to. There is nothing I can do at the moment but drive home, so I just need to focus on that.'

I have worked on this soft skill myself over the past twenty years, learning from mentors and coaches. Sitting with my own emotions is difficult and confronting but it softens them. It stops me in my tracks and gives me the 'pause' moment to not react straight away, but rather to give the feelings the time they need, for me to craft a healthier response. I often worry, for example, that I am not the life of the party. I can't stay up late and can drink very little alcohol as it flares up my CFS and depression, so the words 'you are boring' often dance in. Am I boring because I cannot tell jokes? Because I can't keep up physically? Because every single day I have to train my brain in the morning and tell it I am okay, all is well, and I've got this?

Give yourself some space to try this. Stop the urge to run, hide, bury the emotions and cover them with alcohol, shopping or bouts of aggression towards others that sabotage your own future. The old habits of numbing pain with substances, fighting it, pushing it away, ignoring it, or getting really angry with it often create more problems. None of these are healthy coping strategies that will allow you to heal in the future.

Make a pact with yourself to learn to work with your emotions, to acknowledge them, to allow them to flow through you and guide them for the future. The goal is not to get rid of them, or to stifle or hide them – it is make peace with them in the right context so you can respond and recover with more ease.

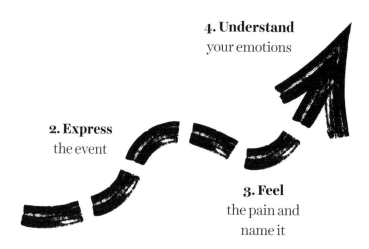

4. Understand
your emotions

2. Express
the event

3. Feel
the pain and
name it

1. Start
where you are

If you are healing and breaking all at once, do not fear, this is growth.

Q. Gibson

Acknowledge Your Feelings and Fear

Once you've made peace with your emotions, taken a breath, sat in the pain and understood the feelings, you can develop your immediate survival plan. Spending time to write up a simple plan with some tasks will give your mind something to focus on and give it some direction. Think of it like a 'break the glass' immediate solution list.

DEVELOP AN IMMEDIATE SURVIVAL PLAN

The survival plan is a temporary quick fix as you navigate what will come next. This is not your forever plan.

Some things you might want to consider addressing in this list are the roles that friends, family, mentors and specialists could play to meet your needs right now. Remember, one day you will tell the story of how you overcame what you are going through now and it will become a part of someone else's survival guide.

I needed an immediate survival plan when I first experienced CFS. I employed a life coach to help me stay positive, and a naturopath to heal my body; I started yin yoga to learn about self-care and the power of breath, which was foreign to me. I also enlisted a couple of friends to be my support crew.

WHAT DO I NEED	WHO CAN SUPPORT ME	HOW AND WHEN
I need a cheerleader to support this new venture	Suzanne, Belinda and Peter	To call and check in on me once a week and negate my self-doubt
I need emotional support to deal with my loss	Michael, Chris and Penny	To walk with each one once a week to get me out of the house and moving and talking
I need to change my brand to fit with the current climate	Harry, Beau and Michelle	To rebrand my offerings and change the website and marketing plan within three weeks
I need legal/accounting advice to sort my affairs	Cam, Steph and Deb	To become financially independent, starting now
I need psychological counselling so that I can minimise stress; not put this stress and sadness on my children	Carolyn, Fiona and David	To arrange weekly appointments throughout this life change
I need to find new interests after I leave this job	Shelley, Sam and Tanya	To nominate new activities for my week so I do not feel I am in an empty void
I need friends to have a relaxing night out with	Melissa, Mel and Alex	Friday-night rosé time!

» Surround yourself with supportive people.
» Know that it is okay to be sad, and happy too.
» Allow yourself to say no to others.
» Know that it's okay to leave events and other gatherings early.
» Have an exit strategy so you can leave when you want to.
» Allow yourself to change your mind.

UNDERSTAND YOUR FEELINGS

Did you know that there is a difference between feelings and emotions? It turns out that feelings are experienced consciously and require mental appraisal and awareness, such as sadness, happiness or irritation. Emotions happen on a physical level and can be conscious or subconscious, such as grief, regret or joy. Our feelings are often messy and feel murky, confusing and overwhelming. Sometimes they are raging and intense, powerful and bold, and sometimes they are quiet, hiding, buried away and hard to recognise.

Feelings are fuelled by a mix of emotions and last a lot longer than our initial emotional outburst. Allow yourself to be true to your feelings, because the more you deny what you feel, the stronger the feelings become.

Putting words to our feelings can be a little overwhelming, so to simplify the process I have a included a chart developed by sociologist Dr Gloria Willcox. It is used to help you understand, communicate and express how you truly feel.

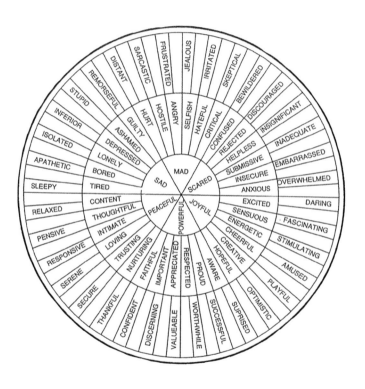

Source: Dr Gloria Willcox (Taylor & Francis Ltd)

The Feeling Wheel provides emotional words that you can use in place of more intellectual ones. Use the wheel to find the word for what you are feeling and build the courage to communicate with both simplicity and authenticity. Here is your guide to using it:

1. **Feel the feeling** – When you start to feel a feeling, look at the wheel.

2. **Identify the core feeling** – Start with the inner section of the wheel and then move outward, moving from core feelings towards further feelings that may be coming up for you.

3. **How do you really feel?** – If the core is not clear for you, you can start from the outside and move inwards to identify the associated feeling and move towards the core emotion. Don't force it, just lightly flow through the words and see what comes up for you.

4. **Compare** – Use the chart to compare how you feel now with how you felt yesterday, or the day before. For example:

*'I am feeling **fearful and insecure** today, but yesterday I felt **content and joyful**.'*

*'I am feeling **happy, powerful and creative** today, but yesterday I felt **stressed and overwhelmed**.'*

Try filling in the blanks here over the course of just one week.

'I am feeling   today, but yesterday I felt   and   .'

'I am feeling   today, but yesterday I felt   and   .'

'I am feeling   today, but yesterday I felt   and   .'

You may find that two or even six different emotions and feelings may come in during one day. You will then see that they flow through you, that change is always happening, that you are not as stuck as you think you may be. Remember: emotions are quick; feelings tend to linger, so we have a chance to try to unpack them and work with them. Note that when you cover up your feelings you restrict your breath, and going back to the conscious use of breath can be an invaluable tool as you learn to express yourself clearly.

Let your feelings move through you. When you untether you will notice that they are forever changing and that tomorrow is a new day. Know that you will feel different, that the current feeling will move through you and you are not so stuck.

When COVID-19 first entered my life and my home state of Victoria went into lockdown, my feelings were intense as I dealt with radical change. As I've mentioned, I could see the opportunity that pivoting could provide and knew how to look for the positive in the situation. Nevertheless, having worked by myself from home for the past twenty years and having perfected the way I structure my day, it was an adjustment. I have my routines, music to put me into the coaching zone, I put the oil burner on and have structured breaks. All of a sudden my husband was working in my home office and my two teen-agers were home schooling. Bye-bye serene work set-up!

I tapped into my emotions and feelings and journalled them, even wrote them on a sticky note on my laptop and recorded each time a big wave of emotion and feeling came in. I noticed that my emotions were erratic, however my feelings were slower. I could easily name and identify them. I could see that they changed up to five times a day. From surprised, to sad, to happy, to excited, to grateful, to fearful about my home situation, my business and career. At the same time as I could see the panic, I could see the gift. A gift to really challenge myself, to get off autopilot, to ask myself the hard questions and to develop what would work best for me: not everyone else, just me.

The Gloria Willcox Feeling Wheel helped me clarify what was happening so I could then prepare how to move forward. Each night at dinner, my family would discuss how we were feeling about the current situation, so we could offer each other support and we could learn to work through it together. There were many gifts, as we all adapted to sharing the one roof again, to really connecting once more.

ASSESS AND TAKE STOCK

It is time to take stock and put ourselves in a better mental and emotional state. As the sheer intensity of the situation you find yourself in starts to recede and you begin to find some calm, you can begin to function again, allow some healing to happen and start to make some plans. To take stock, we need to be in the now, not the past. Bring yourself into the present moment. It is time to ask yourself some powerful questions that start giving you back some control and encourage you to find positive solutions to your unique circumstances. I answer these questions regularly and they truly help me to heal.

WHAT DID I DO TO STRENGTHEN MYSELF TODAY?

E.g. openly communicated with my friends, walked for an hour, journalled, embraced some breathing practice, made a phone call and asked for help.

WHAT SABOTAGING BEHAVIOUR DID I NOTICE TODAY?

E.g. negative self-talk, drank too much alcohol, avoided the problem altogether, compared myself to others, procrastinated.

WHAT DID I LEARN ABOUT MYSELF TODAY?

E.g. that people want to help and support me, that others believe in me more than I do, that walking for half an hour completely changes my state, that sitting still and journalling makes me feel better.

WHAT CAN I IMPROVE FROM TODAY?

E.g. not to judge others as it stops my good energy flow, to drink more water so I am not so lethargic, to write my list for the day so my brain knows what to do.

WHAT TRIGGERS CAME UP FOR ME TODAY?

E.g. hearing about Emily's new job triggered jealousy, hearing about a friend's pregnancy triggered grief as I know that having children is not an option for me.

WHAT WILL I DO NOW TO MOVE FORWARD?

E.g. change my mindset, be kind and gentle to myself and give myself permission to grieve and heal, develop some daily affirmations to help myself move forward.

WHAT AM I GRATEFUL FOR TODAY?

E.g. Sarah brought over some dinner, Bill drove me to my appointment, Peter helped me celebrate my win, I felt happiness today and noticed it.

Developing the habit of taking stock and allowing it to become a way of life is a skill worth developing. A vital part of recovery is allowing yourself to constantly check in with yourself, to reassess and record how you are feeling. It is about putting what you have learnt to good use and consistently looking and finding ways to grow beyond your comfort zone, to allow yourself to evolve and connect to your wisdom.

You need to continually take stock of the situation. You will serve yourself better if you take the time to recognise what is happening and plan a healthy and mindful response.

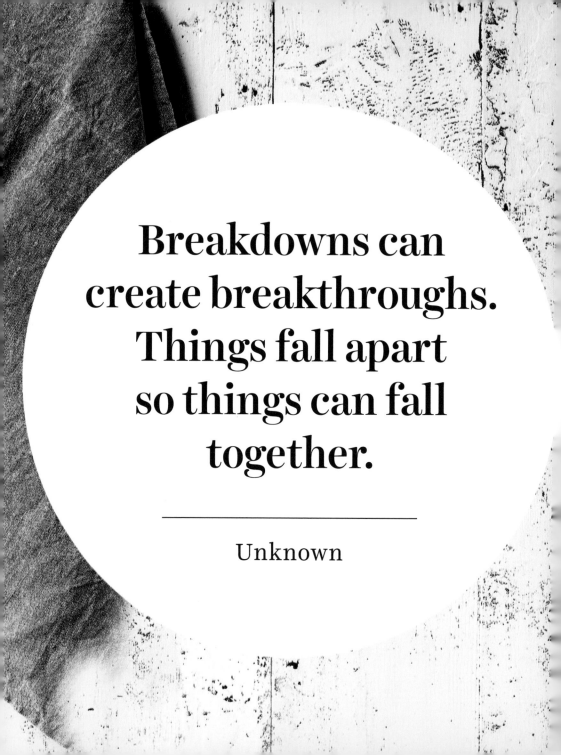

Breakdowns can create breakthroughs. Things fall apart so things can fall together.

———————————

Unknown

DANCE WITH FEAR

Living life with the understanding and acceptance that things can fall apart is one of our most important lessons. My daily vow and invitation to you is to allow yourself to find gratitude for what you still have and not take what you have for granted.

Change can be painful and scary, but it can also be exhilarating. Allowing yourself some room to not know everything is the most important thing of all. We don't know if it is the end of a story or the beginning of a great new adventure.

Change is hard, and messy. But the pain of not changing along with it can be more painful than facing the change and creating a new plan for yourself. Maybe in the long term the change was for the better? Maybe it is forcing you to alter the way you behave, the way you communicate, the way you live your life? It may make you a better person. You may evolve and flourish with this change, which will reveal itself in time. You can stay stuck in the 'falling apart', or you can choose to face the fear so you can fall back together again. I have learnt to embrace the messy middle. I was so black and white, but every day I reminded myself that there is grey in the middle and that I will not feel great each and every day, and I have to be okay with that and work with it.

I often tell my clients that life is like a playground. (The chocolate-box analogy is a little too static for me!) There are many rides, many different options for our lives. We can be on one ride for a while, where it's comfortable, and then choose to step off even though it might seem scary: leave a marriage, start a job or a new business venture. Or you might be enjoying that nice ride – a steady job, a comfy marriage, a home in a special place – and all of a sudden you are thrown off, or the ride breaks down: COVID-19, mid-life crisis, a health scare, a bushfire. You do not have to leave the playground just because one ride is over. There are other rides out there that you haven't tried.

Remember this. You are always in a state of choice. You are never stuck. The next ride you choose to take may not be for forever either. I invite you to be okay with that uncertainty. Don't let fear paralyse you.

Fear is a natural, primitive and very powerful human emotion. It alerts us to the presence of danger, to being in harm's way either physically or psychologically. It can stem from very real threats, or it can be from imagined dangers. I love the acronym FEAR – False, Evidence, Appearing, Real – by James Leslie Payne and use it all the time when fear arises in my day as my mind goes into some old negative thoughts. Speaking in front of large audiences gives me incredible fear, but it is not real and over time I have learnt to challenge it and turn this debilitating fear into some form of excitement.

Our instinct for self-preservation can protect us from repeating past mistakes and experiencing pain, but it can also prevent us from feeling joy, and living life to the fullest.

FOUR STEPS TO SOFTEN YOUR FEAR:

1   **Indulge in self-reflection and positive talk** – When you feel afraid, nervous or anxious, look within to what you are really afraid of. Is it rejection, are you feeling unworthy or perhaps afraid things could be really good? Identify what is at the base of your fear, acknowledge it and then take its hand. Give yourself a pep talk in the mirror about how you deserve to be happy, that you can do this, and that you will be great.

2   **Check in with your options** – Make a list of pros and cons of what would happen if you pursued your visions despite the fear, and then create a list of outcomes if you chose to maintain the status quo.

3   **Take action** – You can take action in the face of fear, without the world crashing down on you. Buddha says, 'A jug fills drop by drop.' Make the call, try that new thing, go back out into the world.

4   **Celebrate** – That you are alive, that you are moving, that things are still changing around you as your healing commences. When you dance with fear, you step closer to feeling whole again.

Everything you want is on the other side of fear.

I dance with fear on a daily basis. Fear of public speaking, fear of a late night (anything after 10 pm puts me in a state of panic because I know the following day may be painful), fear of something happening to a loved one or my children, fear of work drying up. But I also know that fear keeps me on my toes, makes me grateful and challenges me, and I have learnt to flip it quickly.

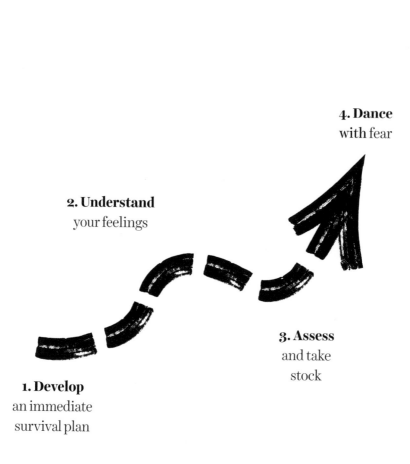

4. **Dance**
with fear

2. **Understand**
your feelings

3. **Assess**
and take
stock

1. **Develop**
an immediate
survival plan

I see your fear, and it's big. I also see your courage, and it's bigger. We can do hard things.

———————————

Glennon Doyle

Untamed

Embrace the Grief

Grief is a natural process when you experience change. As well as grieving through a major life change such as death, divorce and job loss, we can also grieve in more subtle ways – the simple life we left behind when we accepted a new role with a lot more responsibility and remuneration. We can grieve a little and feel excited at the same time. The more significant your loss, the more intense your grief may be.

Grief can affect every part of your life and can be felt in a variety of ways. Your emotions, thoughts, feelings, moods, behaviour, health, your sense of self and personal identity and your relationships with other people can be changed through grief. It can leave you sad, lonely, overwhelmed, stressed, shocked, isolated and numb, or it can sit gently in the background as you move forward, flowing in and out of your soul.

Grief has no set pattern and everyone grieves differently. Some people can grieve for a month and move on, and some may experience bouts of grief for many years. It is through the process of grief that you can begin to create some new experiences, routines, habits and plans that work around your loss.

UNDERSTAND THE STAGES OF GRIEF

There are five main stages of grief: shock and denial, anger, depression and detachment, bargaining, and finally acceptance.

For years I wished I could just give my clients a simple guide to grief, a visual so they could get their bearings. I love this summary of the grief process and I hope you find it helpful.

7. Returning to meaningful life
Empowerment
Security
Self-esteem
Meaning

5. Dialogue and bargaining
Reaching out to others
Desire to tell one's story
Struggle to find meaning
in what has happened

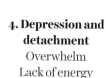

6. Acceptance
Exploring options
A new plan in place

3. Anger
Frustration
Anxiety
Irritation
Embarrassment
Shame

4. Depression and detachment
Overwhelm
Lack of energy
Helplessness

2. Shock and denial
Avoidance
Confusion
Fear
Numbness
Blame

1. 'Normal' functioning

TIPS FOR DEALING WITH GRIEF

» Give yourself permission to grieve.

» Grieve in your own way. There is no right or wrong way, so feel your way through it at your own pace.

» Take care of your physical wellbeing. Stick to the basics of eating, sleeping and moving as you experience the ebb and flow of grief.

» One step at a time. Sometimes it is a case of two steps forward, one step backwards, but know that you will heal with time.

» Understand and familiarise yourself with the different stages of the grief process.

» Recognise your symptoms of grief. These can include waves of emotion, weight loss or gain, insomnia, and feelings of isolation.

» Honour your loss. Journal your thoughts, feelings, emotions, plant a tree, write a poem. It is important to not feel like you have to forget the past: it will always be a part of you, or have a place in your heart, so honour this for yourself.

» Express how you feel with someone you trust. It may be a friend, a counsellor, a mentor, someone you can just be yourself with and express your feelings to without fear of judgement. By letting yourself grieve, you allow the healing to start. Seek refuge and comfort with these people as you move through the stages of grief.

» Be prepared for trigger events – anniversaries, parties, reunions, or gatherings that remind you of your loss. Plan for them and think about how you want to deal with them.

» Get immediate help if you feel you are not coping or are turning to addiction(s) to manage your grief.

» Understand that it takes time, and there is no set period.

I know all the stages of grief. I have been through them myself and I have also held my friends' and clients' hands and supported them through the death of a loved one, marriage breakdowns, friendships failing, business disappointments, a family member suiciding and health issues that cause life and plans to drastically change direction.

PRACTISE RADICAL SELF-COMPASSION

Self-compassion is nutrition for the soul. Self-compassion researcher, author and teacher Dr Kristen Neff describes self-compassion as treating yourself the way you would a best friend. That instead of ignoring your pain with a stiff upper lip, you allow yourself to stop, and tell yourself, 'This is really difficult right now,' and ask, 'How can I comfort and care for myself in this moment?'

Self-compassion is one of the most nurturing and powerful practices we can learn to embrace. Adopting compassion enhances our whole being forevermore. The practice of radical self-compassion can soothe the wounds, take the pressure off and bring in the kindness and empathy that we so deserve. We would always show it for a great friend, but remembering that we are our own best friend and treating ourselves that way makes the healing journey available to us.

My own coach said to me the longest relationship I will ever have is that which I have with myself and my body. When I have thoughts about my body and feel sad and angry about its lack of energy, which I see as a problem and a hindrance, she reminds me to see my body as a child – a child that needs care. She said to stop comparing her to others, to be more kind. My body needs kindness, a loving parent. CFS is my body's way of saying, 'Can you please stop being so mean and demanding and care for me gently?'

Allowing self-compassion in means you care about yourself and want to find some inner harmony. We will all be messy in this period of emotion, feeling, grief, fear and change. We will get frustrated, make mistakes, reach our limit, and fall short of our goals. We are human beings, not human doings: we are not machines but rather a part of nature.

Dr Neff describes the three elements of self-compassion as follows:

1   **'Self-kindness versus self-judgement'**

Knowing that we cannot be perfect, that we may fail and experience difficulties is a part of our journey. Being gentle rather than harshly judging ourselves and others and getting angry and annoyed when we are met with a painful experience is a way to let kindness in the door and allows our emotional agility to improve.

2   **'Common humanity versus isolation'**

Know that all humans go through pain and suffering during life and that it is not just you. All humans make mistakes and can suffer, feel loss, overwhelm or total joy. It is not you alone, so take comfort in the fact that you are not the only one.

3   **'Mindfulness versus over-identification'**

Knowing that being mindful is a non-judgemental state of mind where we can observe our thoughts and feelings as they are. We cannot ignore our feelings and feel compassion for them at the same time. Mindfulness requires you to observe your thoughts and feelings but not get caught up in them. We can notice them and let them pass.

SOME HELPFUL WAYS TO PRACTISE RADICAL SELF-COMPASSION

» **Speak kindly to yourself** – Your words are powerful: talk to yourself as you would to your best friend.

» **Forgive yourself for your mistakes** – This is vital because we all make mistakes. Choose forgiveness and move forward, as you cannot go back to the past.

» **Transform your mindset** – Change your thoughts to accept that sometimes your behaviour is not you. Label your behaviour and open up to the possibility that you can make changes that are far more nurturing.

» **Avoid toxic judgement** – Reserve your negative judgements of situations and others to be more open to future positive possibilities, opportunities and outcomes.

» **Do things that bring you joy** – Allow yourself some happiness, some moments of joy with no guilt. This will help fill your tank.

» **Cultivate your connections with others** – To help care for yourself, connect with others and open up and share your experiences and who you are. You will soon see you are not alone.

» **Care for both your body and mind** – Focus on what makes you feel good and has a positive impact on your mind and body.

» **Uncover passion** – Experiencing change can open up hobbies, new curiosities and new ways of living. Allowing these in without shame or fear can open you up to more balance as you come through the other side of a life-changing event.

» **Remember it's not all about you** – People just want you to be happy. Let go of the need for external validation, as other people are dealing with their own issues and are not sitting at home worrying about yours.

» **Accept that you are not perfect** – Lift the weight off your shoulders by realising that you don't have to be perfect and have it all together.

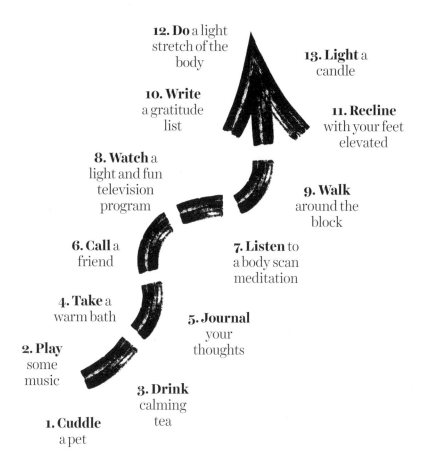

14. BREATHE

12. Do a light
stretch of the
body

13. Light a
candle

10. Write
a gratitude
list

11. Recline
with your feet
elevated

8. Watch a
light and fun
television
program

9. Walk
around the
block

6. Call a
friend

7. Listen to
a body scan
meditation

4. Take a
warm bath

5. Journal
your
thoughts

2. Play
some
music

3. Drink
calming
tea

1. Cuddle
a pet

REPEAT THESE AFFIRMATIONS TO RETRAIN YOUR MIND

I am ready and willing to practise being more compassionate.

I am willing to pause for a fresh new thought, one that serves me better.

I am ready to let some light in.

I close my eyes and leave dark thoughts behind while I enjoy this special space just for me and my breath. One heartbeat at a time, I can feel better.

Whatever it is I'm going through right now, one shift in attention can make a tremendous difference.

Every moment of self-acceptance is a victory.

This journey is rich with purpose.

Self-compassion helps me respond to stress in creative and fruitful ways.

I am kind to myself because the more love I give to myself, the more love I breathe into my life. This perspective feeds my dreams, goals, desires and needs.

I love the phrase 'radical self-compassion'. It means so much to me. To be gentle with myself, to deeply care for myself, to be there for my family, friends and clients, I must show up authentically. Through courses and reading many, many books, and working with some wellbeing mentors and coaches over the years, I finally understand this superpower – compassion. I am so harsh and critical of myself, I expect so much of myself that I burn out all the time. Learning this has really changed my life; it has allowed me to find a pace that works for my career, mental health and wellbeing.

CHOOSE YOUR PATH WITH CARE

Now that you have your breath and you have found some space, think about how you may want to handle the situation in future. It is time to help yourself, to develop, build and introduce some resilience and hardiness and choose your path with care, rather than with reckless abandon. Be aware that blame will not help you: it will leave you feeling victimised, stuck and anchored in the grief process.

It is now a process of figuring out what life can look like when it's not going to the original plan. Start to plant some seeds in your mind with these questions:

What is next?

How can I let joy in the door?

Sheryl Sandberg carefully chose her words, thoughts and actions after her husband died suddenly, detailed in her book *Option B*. When she was asked how she kept going, she told the story of a woman she'd just met who was an artist and a widow. 'Someone asked her how she kept doing her work, and she said, "Because the rest of the parts of me didn't die." She said, "I'm a widow, but I'm still a mother, and I'm still an artist." . . . If you can't find moments of joy and let yourself be happy, your kids can't be happy.'

THERE ARE THREE WAYS TO CHOOSE YOUR PATH TO MOVE FORWARD:

» Be devastated by the incident, come away feeling depressed, worried and feeling a failure.

» Try to bounce back to how you were before the event.

» Bounce forward, allowing yourself to learn from the negative event. Allow yourself to feel the change, normalise it and not be too hard on yourself.

After my last bout of depression, I sought further positive changes. I worked harder with the naturopath to get off the antidepressants, as they made my chest feel tight (note you must consult your doctor before coming off antidepressants as there can be serious side effects), and to find another substitute. I committed to go deeper into being kinder to myself, to practise non-judgement and to keep my eyes on my own plate and not compare myself to others. I went to another level of kindness and compassion for myself and others. I embraced that I am unique and not a human doing but a human being: my body is my home, it houses my soul – I will guide it and train it, but I will accommodate some of the feed-back it gives me.

Can you open yourself up to feeling stronger? That if you can live through this, you can live through anything? That you can become more grateful now, that you have new relationships, that you have received more support than you thought possible, and now you are closer to others than you were before?

Sandberg said, 'Post-traumatic growth doesn't mean that it's overall more positive. I would trade all the growth to have Dave back. But I'm closer with my parents than I was. I'm closer with my closest friends than I was. I have more appreciation. I have more perspective.'

Quick check-in

What new things am I learning
about myself and others?

Who has supported me?
Which person has been surprising?

What new opportunities have arisen
from the life-changing event?

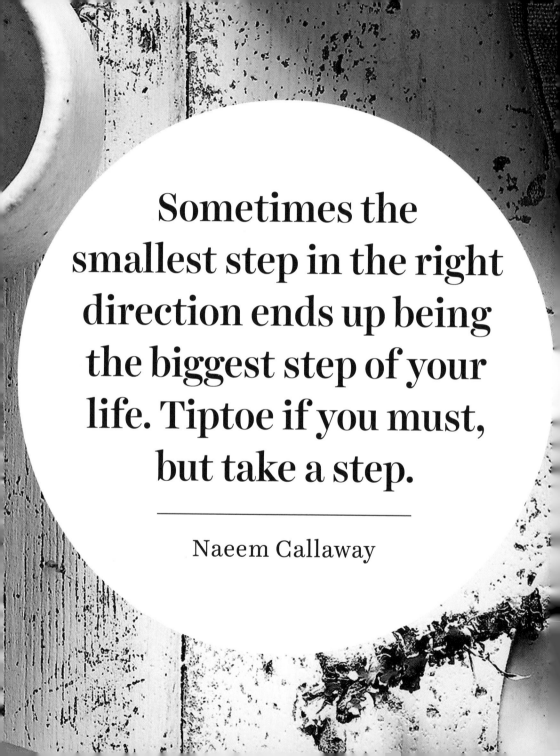

Sometimes the smallest step in the right direction ends up being the biggest step of your life. Tiptoe if you must, but take a step.

Naeem Callaway

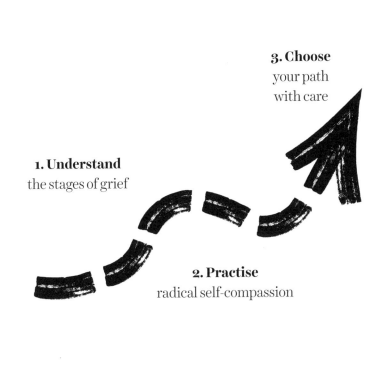

1. Understand
the stages of grief

2. Practise
radical self-compassion

3. Choose
your path
with care

Choose Your Narrative

It is time to change, adapt and make Plan B. Let's get clear on what your story is so that you can own it. You are not only going to tell this story to yourself, but to others too, so you need to frame it in a way that you feel comfortable with.

WHAT'S YOUR STORY?

Rewriting your story is not about denial or pretending nothing really changed, but about finding some meaning in the events of your life and accepting that those events made you the person you are now.

> » Remember that you are the editor of your life's story.
> » Ask if your story is true and whether it makes you feel alive or shuts you down.
> » Practise self-appreciation – add some positive elements to your story.
> » Leave your old story behind.

Anyone can change their story if it is not working for them. The first step is to realise that you have one, the next is to challenge your beliefs about it and the final step is to re-author your life's journey. The meaning that we give our past, or the events that change our lives, matters. This is how our story gets created. When you choose to reframe, reinterpret and rewrite the narrative of it, its role then allows you to become more powerful and things start to change.

Any painful life event gives you the opportunity to define yourself as a victim or a survivor – which do you choose to be?

Byron Katie, author of *Loving What Is* and teacher of the self-enquiry method known as 'The Work', recommends that we write down our thoughts and judgements of our current reality, then systematically challenge each of them to uncover the underlying beliefs that are holding us back. Once you have written your core belief about what is holding you back, answer the following questions:

Is it 100 per cent true?
Can I absolutely know that it's true?
How do I react when I think the thought?
Who would I be without the thought?

OLD STORY	NEW STORY	HOW IT MAKES ME FEEL
I racked up a lot of credit card debt.	I have credit card debt that I will repay with renewed focus.	I feel back in control.
I lost my marriage because I wasn't good enough.	My marriage was a lesson to communicate better. I will learn from this and find a healthier relationship.	I have learnt a lesson to make me a better person.
My ex and his family are doing everything they can to destroy me.	I am working to legally financially separate, create a great parenting plan and be the best mother I can be. It's a brand-new life.	I feel disappointed but I am okay.
COVID-19 has ruined my thriving business and I am shattered. It's not fair.	My business had to shut but the time and space have allowed for a reset, to reconnect with my family, and I am now creating a new online business that is pandemic-proof.	I am adaptable, I can pivot, it may work out better than before.
My business partner ripped me off.	I am reconfiguring the business so that it can continue and I have learnt some amazing lessons.	I am more conscious now, a better business operator, and take responsibility for the finances.
I no longer have an executive role and I hate not having the status that goes with that.	I loved my leadership role but now it is time for new challenges.	I have a new CV, a new LinkedIn profile and I am ready for the next opportunity.
My dog has been my best friend. He died in my arms and I just can't get over it.	I am working through the five stages of grief and slowly letting go of the sadness.	Now that I do not have to care for a dog I have a lot more freedom to travel and I am doing pilates teacher training as a new focus.

Your ultimate goal is to feel free in life without any story at all, and to remember that reality is often a lot kinder than the story you tell yourself.

Social psychologist and Harvard lecturer Dr Amy Cuddy advises people to stand in a power pose – a wide stance, with broad shoulders and hands on your hips – for a couple of minutes a day, especially when an old story starts playing in your head. By doing this she asserts that you can change the levels of cortisol and testosterone in your body in just two minutes. These hormones are associated with both power and stress, and this will enable you to tell your story with more confidence.

DEALING WITH OTHERS

Dealing with other people when you are ready can be quite confronting and can trigger a whole range of emotions if you are not prepared. Go gently as you venture back out into the world, take some time to think about how you want to deal with others, and how you can express yourself and your wants and needs to them.

QUICK TIPS

1   HAVE YOUR DAILY KEYNOTE READY

For example, 'It's an amicable separation and we wish each other well. We think it's best for both of us. Our son is happier having so much one-on-one time with us.'

'It was a great role but I am not missing the 6 am flights to Sydney.'

2   ISSUE YOUR CALL TO ACTION

The call to action steers the conversation away from the 'why' of the event, and towards a 'what's next?' For example, 'It would be great if you could come and help me redecorate my lounge room.'

'It would be great if we could have a regular walk together every Monday to get me out of the house.'

3   ALWAYS BE CLOSING

Your 'closer' gets you out of the conversation before you say anything you might regret, or steers the other person away from the topic if you are not feeling up to talking about it. The idea is to deflect the conversation back to them immediately if you don't want to discuss all that has happened to you in the local supermarket. For example, 'Thanks for asking. What's new with you?', 'Thanks for asking – and how is your family going?' Remember, people will stop asking questions if you give them a chance to talk about themselves.

MY KEYNOTE IS:

_____

_____

MY CALL TO ACTION IS:

_____

_____

MY CLOSING IS:

_____

_____

Practise these a few times so you feel comfortable in any situation.

Be prepared to hear what you may not want to hear, as people put their own feelings and opinions onto your experience, and be ready to deflect to protect your energy when you are not feeling up to talking about it.

When my client's marriage broke down everyone kept saying to her, 'Oh, how are you, are you okay?' and would want to know all the details. We worked together to form a daily keynote along the lines of, 'Thanks for asking, it is a tough road and I am taking it day by day at the moment. But more importantly, how are you? What is happening in your world?'

STAY CONNECTED

When we are experiencing change in our lives, we can tend to isolate ourselves, and feel more comfortable hiding rather than facing the world. This insularity can have a negative impact on our confidence and the challenge is to keep ourselves moving out in the world. I always tell myself to get comfortable with feeling uncomfortable, for although I am a speaker on a large stage, I am quite an introvert and am very happy in my own company, not seeing anyone. I have no idea why I enjoy speaking on stage (the love of sharing knowledge, tools and tips to help others is what drives me) but I am happy with a simple life, being at home and feeling safe.

The easiest way to stay connected is to develop some weekly routines with friends, family or colleagues, or some regular sessions with your mentor, coach or counsellor. Pick three or four regular activities to help you stay connected, even when you don't feel like it, as they could be the best medicine for you until you are fully back on your feet. Your routine may look something like this:

MONDAY   Start the day with a morning walk with a positive friend

TUESDAY   Coffee with a family member

WEDNESDAY   Day to yourself, other than your immediate work and family commitments

THURSDAY   Movie night with the family

FRIDAY   End-of-week drinks with some supportive friends

SATURDAY   Dinner out with a friend

SUNDAY   A bike ride during the day and an early night

Or you may develop some deeper long-term friendship traditions such as going to the Comedy Festival every year with the same friends or doing the same fun run each year with the same group, so you have some touch points throughout the year.

THIS TOO SHALL PASS

Remember that whatever you are feeling and experiencing will pass. 'This too shall pass' reflects the temporary nature of the human condition. I have these words up on my mirror to remind me that however I am feeling will pass, it will not stay the same. This goes for elation and joy, as well as sadness and pain. Nothing is permanent in this world – everything changes and moves constantly.

The truth is, everything will be okay, as soon as you are okay with everything. And that's the only time everything will be okay
– Michael Singer

'This too shall pass' allows us to note that the universe is constantly on the move, giving us confidence that we will not stay in a state of stress for too long and reminding us of the bigger picture. These words allow me to not hold on too tightly, to allow the feelings and emotions to flow through me, just like a river.

5. **Choose**
your narrative

4. **Embrace** the grief

2. Stop. **Breathe.**

3. **Acknowledge** your
feelings and fear

1. The **change**

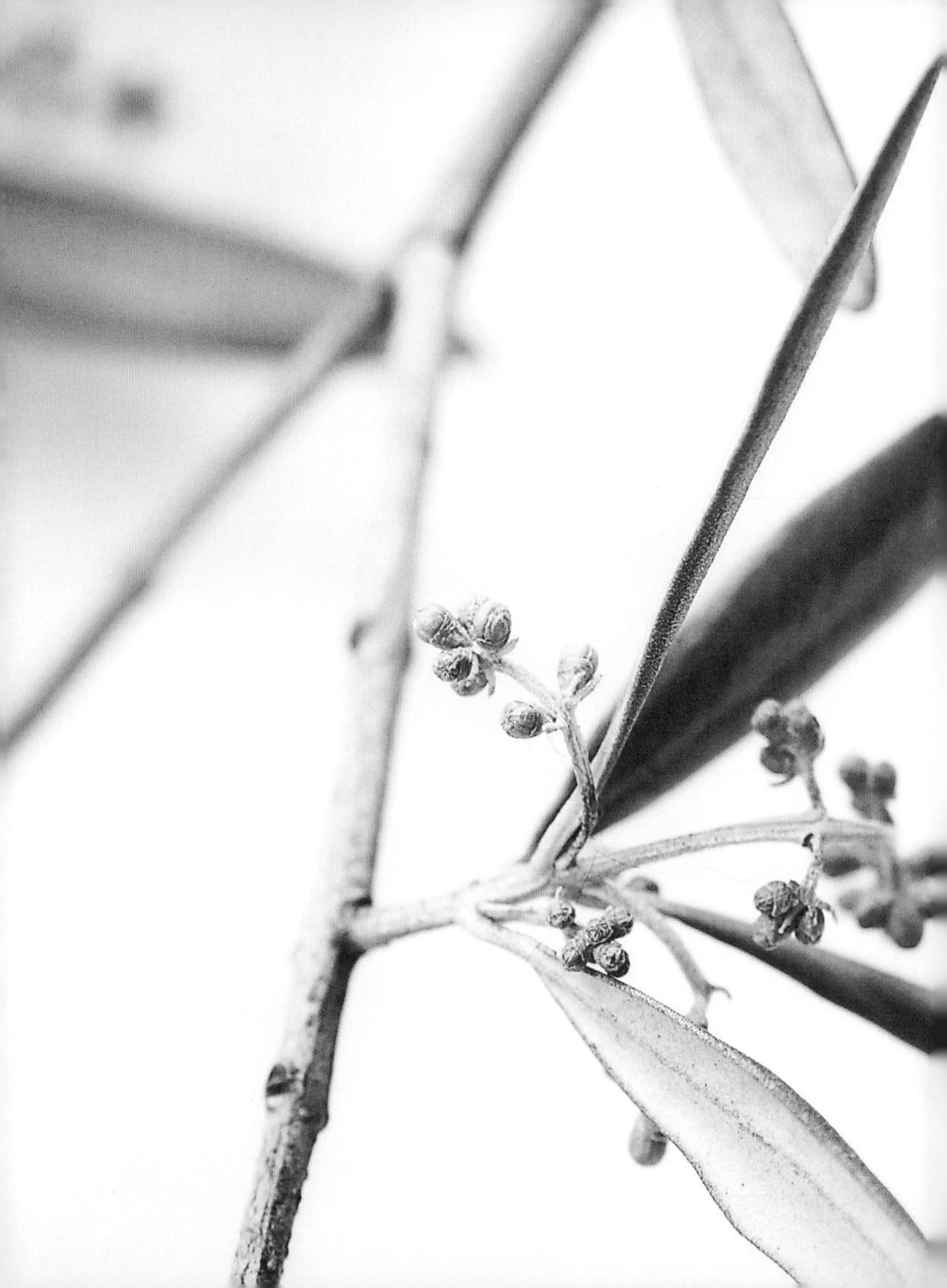

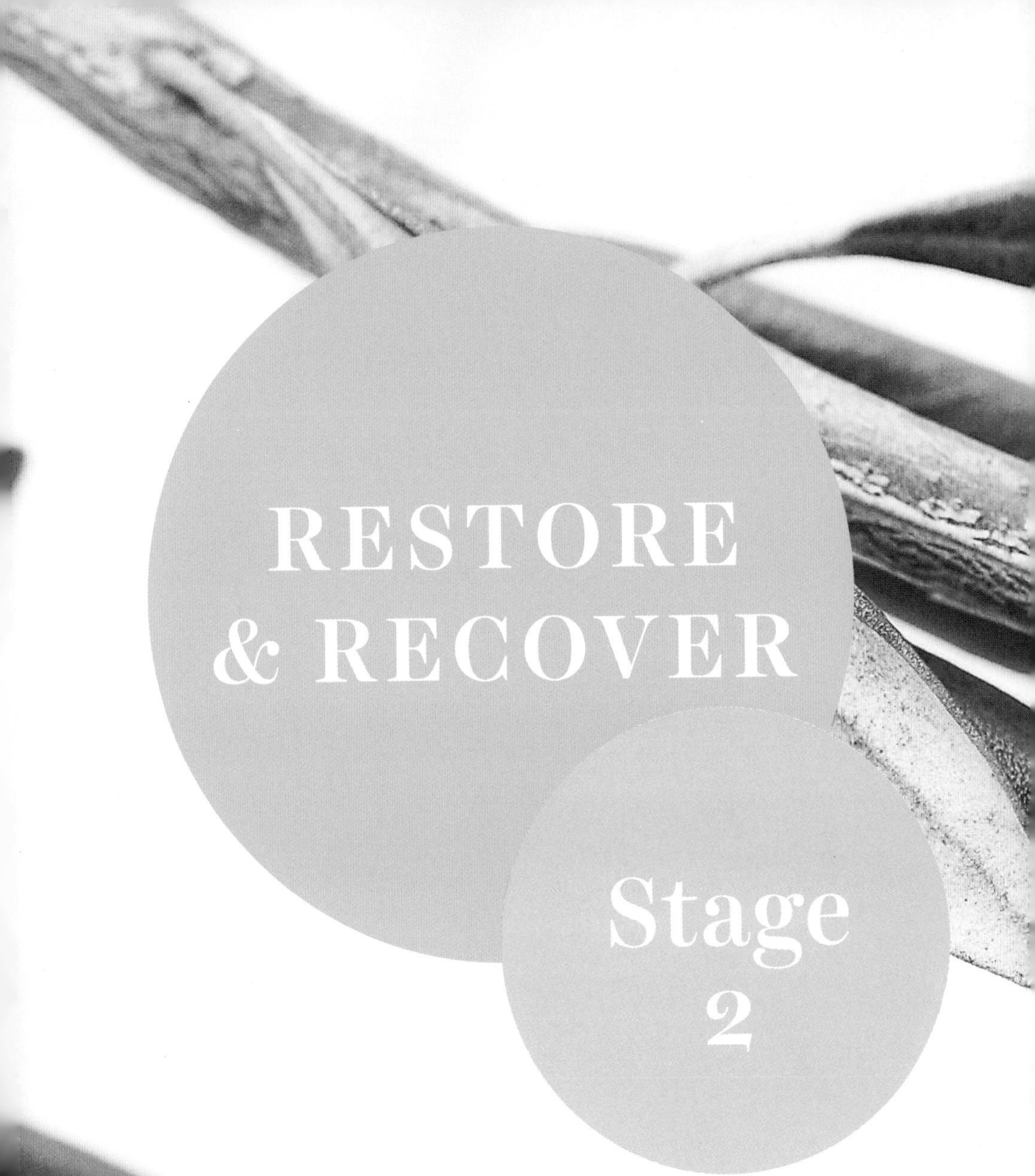

RESTORE & RECOVER

Stage 2

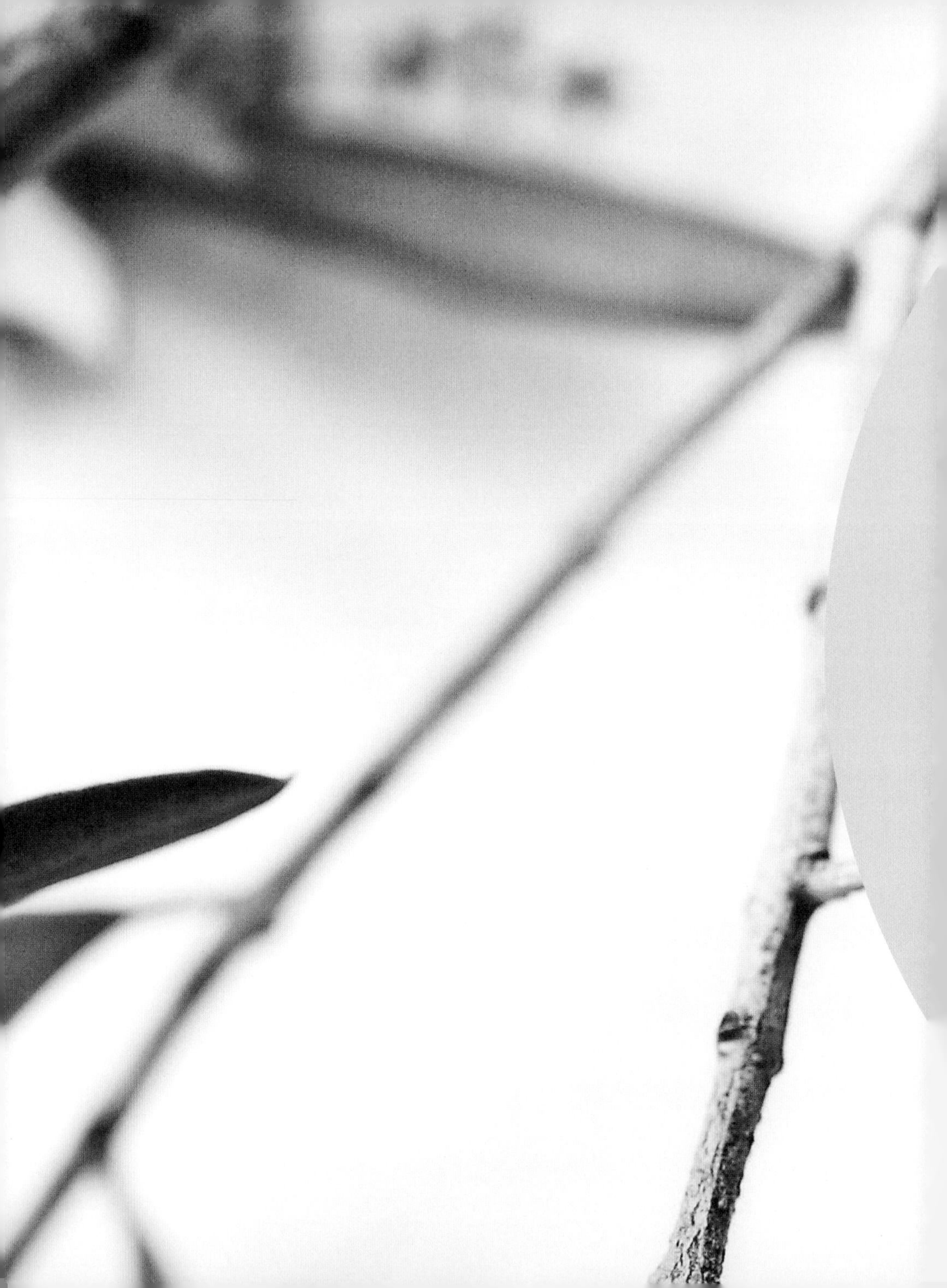

Stage 2

RESTORE & RECOVER

THE HEALING

SINK INTO SELF-CARE 86

Bathe in extreme self-care

Master your calm with self-connection and breath

Move through overwhelm with FLOW and RAIN

RENEW AND REFUEL 108

Restore your four pillars of health

Establish supportive routines and rituals

Heal through mindfulness

OPEN THE PATH TO POSITIVITY 133

Practise loving-kindness (metta)

Give yourself permission to let go

Start saying yes!

Flow and identify the gift

RELINQUISH THE PAST – YOU'VE GOT THIS 149

Celebrate the small wins

Find patience and hope

Set small timelines

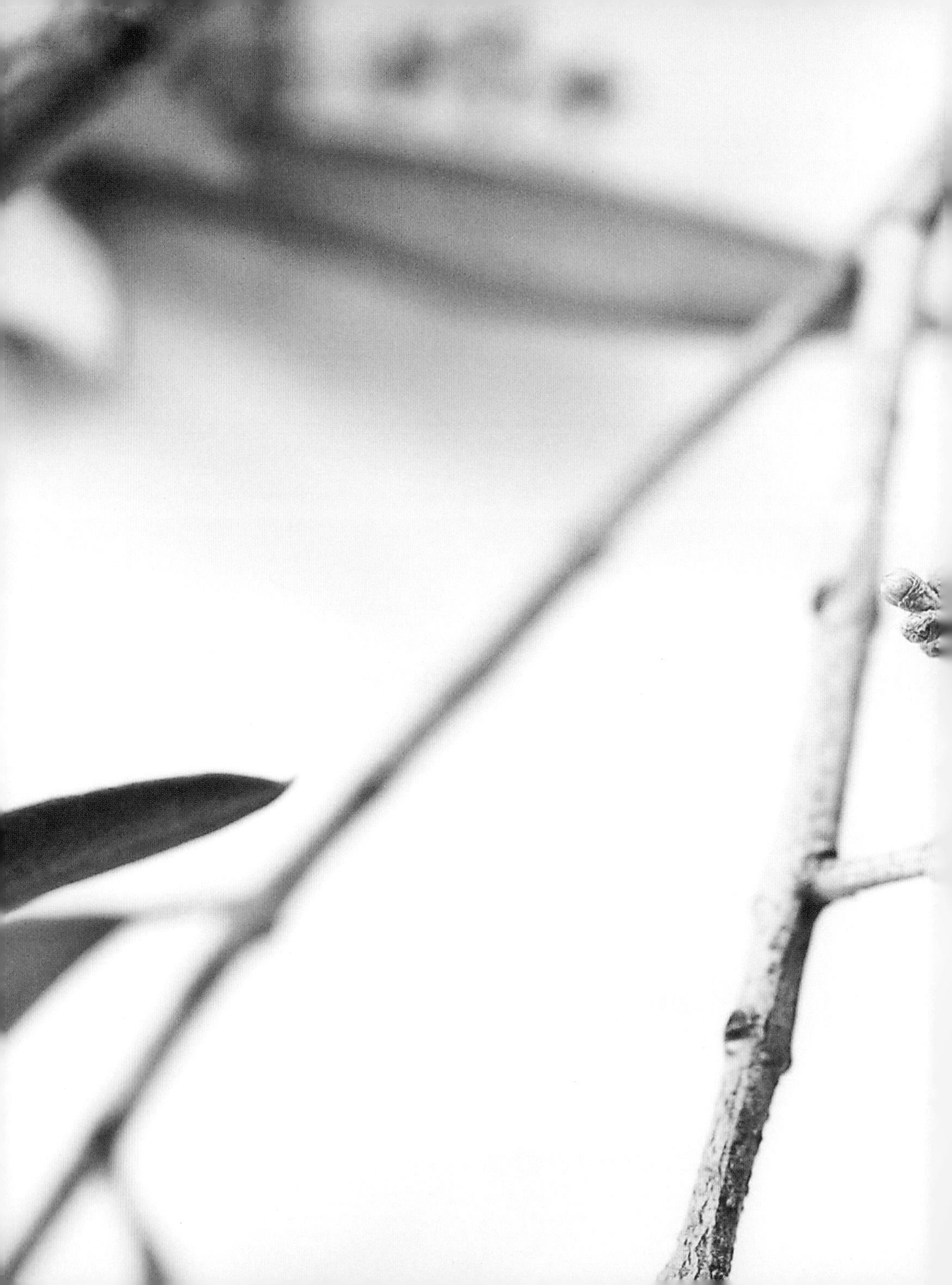

You do not see me for I am hidden inside the soul. Others want you for themselves, but I call you back to yourself.

The second stage is to gently adapt to your current situation, to recover and find new energy before you prepare to make new, longer-term plans. This is the time to make space for yourself, embrace some solitude, and sink into self-soothing practices to fill up your depleted physical and emotional fuel tanks.

It takes time – precious, slow time – to restore, renew and reprioritise yourself. In this chapter I will give you the most powerful, trusted and time-tested healing practices to help you reconnect with yourself, repair the damage, find your balance, open the door to positivity, and feel some little wins.

It is easy to get stuck in a self-pity funk. But this is an opportunity to take ownership of your situation, to unlearn some of your old habits and routines and establish new ones. Patience is your friend, time will heal you, and you may even identify some gifts along the way. So focus on the basics, make room for kindness, and remember that from little things, big things grow.

4. Relinquish the past – you've got this

Celebrate the small wins

Find patience and hope

Set small timelines

2. Renew and refuel

Restore your four pillars of health

Establish supportive routines and rituals

Heal through mindfulness

3. Open the path to positivity

Practise loving-kindness (metta)

Give yourself permission to let go

Start saying yes!

Flow and identify the gift

1. Sink into self-care

Bathe in extreme self-care

Master your calm with self-connection and breath

Move through overwhelm with FLOW and RAIN

Sink Into Self-Care

Self-care means giving yourself permission to pause. It will restore you so you can give the world the best of yourself once again. It is an essential part of healing and recovery. So take a stretch, wrap yourself up and sink right into the beautiful practice of self-care.

BATHE IN EXTREME SELF-CARE

Intentional rest is a powerful pause. Rest turns you from a human doing into a human being. It is the secret to recovery and embracing the power of change, and it will take you from stress to stillness. Rest creates the space for automatic healing and rebalancing.

I used to think of rest as a weakness. Whenever I stopped and rested, especially as a mum, I felt so guilty, weak and pathetic. But now I think of rest as a drink stop on the marathon of life that all of us are running. Why not stop regularly for short breaks to refuel, review and reset so you can enjoy and get the most out of the race?

When I travel to speak at conferences, I don't go out and party but rather take the opportunity to invest in self-care. I go to bed with a meditation at 8.30 pm so I can get up early and discover the city on foot. When the kids were smaller, I would finish work at 3 pm and then would give myself permission to lie down for twenty minutes on weekdays before school pick-up to do a deep-rest meditation, with Rex, my dog. This was and is my pause, my circuit breaker, my little top-up before the kids get home from school and my husband gets home from work. I need to rest so I can get dinner prepared, listen to their how their days were, assist with homework if needed, and have the energy for great conversations over the dinner table. On days when I don't stop and rest – when it just doesn't happen because 'life gets in the way' – by the end of the day I feel deeply exhausted.

Remember that sleep alone is not enough. The richest of fuel comes from the practice of rest. It is one of the fundamental needs of the human body, yet many people don't make time for it, and instead become habituated to feeling overworked, overwhelmed and exhausted. But if your tank is empty, it will be difficult for you to find clarity and make positive decisions down the track. Rest is sacred – our minds, bodies and souls need it. If you cannot rest, it is because you haven't stopped running.

Resting is sometimes referred to as a quiet wakefulness – the feeling of a wave of calm washing over you as you close your eyes, put your feet up and clear your mind for a moment. It lets your muscles and organs relax, reduces your stress, can improve your mood, and increases your alertness, creativity, motivation and mental clarity. It doesn't take much, but it is incredibly powerful. Give yourself permission to try it.

These breaks don't need to be long, just five to twenty minutes of your day. You have seventy-two blocks of twenty minutes each day, so why not dedicate one of these to intentional rest? It will allow you to better handle the overwhelm, the grief and the emotions that are still flowing in and out of you. You don't have to lie down to rest – you can do breath work, meditate, listen to calming music, or even just daydream, while seated. But whatever you do, make it your challenge to master deliberate rest.

SOME IDEAS FOR INTENTIONAL RESTING

» Take a warm bath.

» Relax with a massage.

» Go for a gentle stroll.

» Incorporate essential oils into your routine.

» Find a place to be still – a comfortable chair, a spot in the garden.

» Plant a tree and nurture it.

» Sit and listen to some soothing music.

» Listen to a guided meditation.

» Take some time to cuddle a pet.

» Practise not thinking by tapping into your senses: sight, hearing, touch, taste, smell.

WHAT WOULD LOVE DO?

When you need to rest, ask yourself, 'What would love do?' Sit with this powerful question and see what comes up for you. It will give you deeper insight into what you need right now and will allow you to honour yourself once again. I have this question on my wall so as to never forget it. It guides me on a daily basis, especially if I am feeling impatient or agitated.

Now my kids are older, I take twenty minutes every day to intentionally rest, to do a guided meditation or sit in silence in my special chair in the backyard. This is my promise to myself, my non-negotiable mini 'me' moment that gives me space to think, practise mindfulness, and find peace, kindness and gratitude.

You can be fully engaged in life, but you need to strategically disengage to practise rest.

THINGS I'D LIKE TO START DOING ON A REGULAR BASIS

1.

2.

3.

4.

5.

What would love do right now?

SOME QUICK PROMPTS FOR YOUR JOURNAL ENTRY

I FEEL . . .

....

I WOULD LIKE . . .

....

I FORGIVE . . .

....

I FIND JOY IN . . .

....

I BELIEVE . . .

....

Sometimes the most important thing in a whole day is the rest we take between two deep breaths.

Etty Hillesum

MASTER YOUR CALM
WITH SELF-CONNECTION
AND BREATH

Slow down – inhale peace, exhale worry

It is often said that deep breaths are like little love notes to yourself. They offer you a pause, reconnection and recovery. The quality of your days reflects the quality of your breath. Breathing is like medicine for your soul and invites calmness and richness back into your world.

Practising deep breathing allows me to live with joy, energy and inspiration. It allows me to see my CFS and depression as gifts, without which I would be living a life devoid of fulfilment, rushing from experience to experience without fully taking everything in. Breathing gives me calmness and confidence; it gives me the ability to listen properly to my family, friends and clients and serve them to the best of my ability. It helps me to slow down and truly feel what I am doing. I have written about breathing in every book I have published as it is the source of life, our refuge, and an incredibly important part of recovery.

In coaching sessions, I am guided by clients' breathing. I often ask them to slow their speech, to take a breath, so we can work out how they are really feeling and what is really going on. 'How are you?' and 'How are you really?' are two very different questions with very different answers.

I have worked with many high achievers, including elite athletes and CEOs. They respect the power of three breaths; they see this as their superpower. I teach them to constantly reset, to take three breaths before making their next commitment, to ensure it feels right in their belly and not just their mind. We take three breaths to really ground ourselves when exploring solutions, finding clarity for the future and connecting with our higher selves.

Dolly Parton once said that storms make trees take deeper roots. When your mind is surging with a storm front of emotions –

volatility, fear, anger and overwhelm – your breath can serve as your anchor, your lifeline. When it feels like gusts of emotion are sweeping you away, imagine yourself strong and grounded as a tree, your trunk steady, your roots deep in mother earth even as your branches thrash wildly in the wind and rain. Breathing deeply, with a focus on exhaling, will help you to find your centre and weather the storm you are facing.

I give you permission to stop and breathe

Storms make trees take deeper roots.

Dolly Parton

Dirga pranayama is the art of controlled breathing. The word 'prana' refers not only to breath, but also to air and life itself. Three breaths is all it takes, and you can do this anywhere at any time. It is your secret weapon – so master it, practise it, and give yourself this precious practice.

Take three long, deep breaths. As you continue to inhale and exhale, you might add a few words, such as these from Thich Nhat Hanh:

Breathing in I smile
Breathing out I relax
This is a wonderful moment

Or even quite simply:

I am breathing in quietly
I am breathing out deeply

I breathe in light
I breathe out and let go

Your breath is your greatest teacher, your greatest friend, your connection back to your home, your soul. To calm yourself, breathe out for longer than you breathe in.

MOVE THROUGH OVERWHELM WITH FLOW AND RAIN

You will no doubt have days where you feel okay, and other days where you are in a slump. This is where you may want to allow the word FLOW into your life. Let everything flow through you like water in a river. There is no need to tire yourself out or cause yourself more pain and suffering by trying to stop the current. You can surrender.

I have the word FLOW on my bathroom mirror, and occasionally set it as a screensaver, to remind myself to embody this mindset. Once I have my goals and my to-do list for the day, I try my best to flow through them; to flow like a river and not get stuck behind boulders, knowing that not everything will run smoothly and that I may need to be more patient. When anxiety comes to town, or overwhelm floods in, RAIN, coined by Michele McDonald, is also here to help. It is a simple yet powerful four-step mindfulness practice that you can incorporate into your wellbeing toolkit at any point in life. If you are yearning for clarity and deeper connection, RAIN can help you work through intense and difficult thoughts and emotions.

Recognise what is
happening (roots of
understanding)

Nurture with self-
compassion (awakens
love)

Allow the experience
to be just as it is
(grounds of love)

Investigate with
gentle attention,
interest and
care (deepens
understanding)

Psychologist Tara Brach is a great advocate of RAIN and describes it as follows:

> *RAIN* directly de-conditions the habitual ways in which you resist your moment-to-moment experience. It doesn't matter whether you resist what is by lashing out in anger, by having a cigarette, or by getting immersed in obsessive thinking. Your attempt to control the life within you and around you cuts you off from your own heart and from this living world.

I use RAIN in so many parts of my life. You can too. I'll show you how it works.

When feelings of stress and anxiety kick in, or your body goes into fight-or-flight mode – when you have a big decision to make, or a problem comes up at work – how you react is important. Your first instinct is probably to think unpleasant thoughts, to be negative, rather than sit in the truth of what is happening. But let it RAIN.

FILL IN YOUR RAIN CHART

R = RECOGNISE

Recognise without judgement the emotions and thoughts you are experiencing. Just notice and name them and then say to yourself: 'Oh, so that's what's on your mind. Remember this too shall pass.' Some R examples: I really am craving chocolate; every time my son leaves the house I panic that something will happen to him; I really am terrified about doing this work presentation as I am scared of public speaking; what if I meet my ex-husband's new girlfriend in the local supermarket?

....

....

....

....

A = ALLOW, ACCEPT AND ACKNOWLEDGE

Allow your discomfort and accept it as your present reality. You may not like it, but you are facing it. Some examples: Ah yes, I am worried about that again; I am anxious about being by myself again; I am lonely; I am scared. Hear these and allow them to be just as they are.

....

....

....

....

I = INVESTIGATE AND INQUIRE WITH GENTLE ATTENTION

Ask yourself: What caused this? Is there another occasion when I've felt this way? What thoughts do I associate with these feelings? How realistic is my thinking? What do I need? How can I help myself or someone else? These questions deepen your understanding and allow you to take action.

....

....

....

....

N = NURTURE WITH SELF-COMPASSION

Show yourself understanding, friendliness and generosity, like you would a loving partner. This is not self-pity but rather acceptance of your humanity, your imperfection and your change in circumstances.

....

....

....

....

In her book *Radical Acceptance*, Tara Brach puts it this way: 'Instead of resisting our feelings of fear and grief, we embrace our pain with the kindness of a mother holding her child.' This is a practice you can try.

RAIN will set you free and wash away negative thoughts; it will take you from overwhelm to gentle compassion.

Feeling overwhelmed?

A HELPFUL CHECKLIST

Relax your shoulders

Take three breaths

Do a body-scan meditation

List your top three priorities

Take a break

Go for a walk

Adjust your schedule

Ask for help

Remember: you can handle this

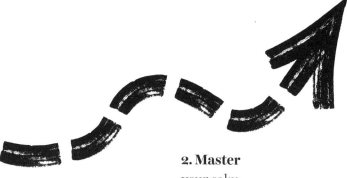

3. Move
through overwhelm
with FLOW and RAIN

2. Master
your calm
with self-
connection and
breath

1. Bathe
in extreme
self-care

The first wealth is health.

Ralph Waldo
Emerson

Renew and Refuel

RESTORE YOUR FOUR PILLARS OF HEALTH

Your body and mind are your most valuable possessions. Your health is your wealth; however, your health is not just whether or not you feel good today. It is a wonderful holistic system with so many interconnected elements. If you want to fully restore yourself, you need to get to know the four main pillars of health: mental, emotional, physical and spiritual.

Health is my number-one value. It is my home base, what I work for every day – my boss. So I start each day by asking myself what I will do for my mental, emotional, physical and spiritual health. I add these things as actionable items on my to-do list, alongside my other personal and work-related goals. Meditating, walking, hydrating, journalling, practising gratitude and helping others are all on my to-do list – daily!

When Peta, a burnt-out single parent, left her highly stressful high-paying job as a medical device salesperson to live a life more aligned with her values, she had a big breakdown. Her workplace was so toxic she had decided she could not continue working there. In our coaching sessions, we started with the basics – her values and her health. By understanding the four pillars of health she was able to build a pathway to healing and ultimately thriving.

The body heals with play, the mind heals with laughter, and the spirit heals with joy.

Arthur Ashe

To lay a strong foundation for the future, restore your four pillars of health. Design a plan that works for you, using the following prompts:

MENTAL – YOUR MIND – To think, learn and grow. What are you doing for your mental health?

EMOTIONAL – YOUR HEART – To love and care for yourself and others. What are you doing for your emotional health?

PHYSICAL – YOUR BODY – To eat, move, sleep and breathe. What are you doing for your physical health?

SPIRITUAL – YOUR SOUL – To connect with purpose and a sense of belonging. What are you doing for your spiritual health?

Make an intentional list for yourself – a self-care inventory. Plan at least a few weeks ahead so you don't have to constantly add to the list. It will serve as your guide, help you when you feel stuck, and gently allow you to move forward.

MENTAL HEALTH

BASIC IDEAS LIST	MY LIST
Write in my journal	
Practise positive affirmations	
Read ten pages of a lighthearted book	
Do a twenty-minute guided meditation	
Take a mental health day	
Declutter a drawer or cupboard/tidy up	
Book an appointment with my therapist or life coach	

EMOTIONAL HEALTH

BASIC IDEAS LIST	MY LIST
Ask for help	
Spend time with people who care	
Do something I love	
Speak to myself in the mirror the way I would speak to my best friend	
Be open to receiving love from others	
Write in my journal	
Do a creative activity	

PHYSICAL HEALTH

BASIC IDEAS LIST	MY LIST
Drink two litres of water per day	
Move my body for one hour per day	
Get eight hours of sleep each night	
Rest for twenty minutes each day	
Eat wholefoods	
Take any necessary supplements	
Set some tech-free time each day	

SPIRITUAL HEALTH

BASIC IDEAS LIST	MY LIST
Write a nightly gratitude list	
Visualise my older self and embrace the wisdom I hear from them	
Have faith in myself and act with integrity	
Set meaningful goals for the day	
Learn how my chakra system works	
Volunteer my help	
Be authentic all day and work for my core values	

Mastering others is strength; mastering yourself is true power.

Lao Tzu

Self-care is your best business plan. Keep a master list of your mental, emotional, physical and spiritual self-care practices in your journal, so you can remind yourself of them all the time. Place your favourite quotes and positive affirmations on the mirror so they greet you each morning. Put your main goal and affirmation for the day on a sticky note on the car dashboard or next to your laptop, to remind yourself to stay focused on this.

Quick check-in

WHEN I FEEL	IT MEANS
Insecure	I am human
Empty	It's time to fill my tank
Stuck	I am forcing clarity
Confused	I am scared to choose
Lost	I am on the verge of a breakthrough

ESTABLISH SUPPORTIVE ROUTINES AND RITUALS

I love working with clients to establish a simple and supportive framework for intentional living and intensive self-care. Routines and rituals help you to feel in control, provide fulfilment, and leave you nourished and nurtured. For the sake of self-care, it can be helpful to make a distinction between the two, with routines being everyday tasks that need to be completed, and rituals being actions that bring meaning, learning and even joy to your life. By simply changing the way you think about them, you can turn your routines into rituals. It is all about your mindset.

For example, to turn doing the washing from a routine into a ritual, I made the laundry a space I enjoy spending time in. By adding nice plants to the room and putting inspiring quotes on the walls, I created an organised space where I can breathe, take things slowly and mindfully, feel gratitude for having washing to do, for the washing machine, and for the environment I have set up. I often stay in there for longer than I have to and use it to have a mini 'me' moment, to take three deep breaths to calm and reground myself.

Similarly, unstacking the dishwasher used to be a mundane chore until I trained myself to do it mindfully and with gratitude, giving thought to how lucky I am to have a family to eat with that created dishes to be washed.

Daily routines are not usually motivating, because we tend to view them as chores. On the other hand, daily rituals offer us meaning, energy and enjoyment, and give us a sense of purpose as they nourish our four pillars of health. Looking after a plant, for instance, can be a mundane routine, or you can tend to it mindfully and lovingly, find pleasure in it and feel reverence as it thrives and flowers.

Make an effort to get back to the basics and focus on what is essential for you. Challenge yourself to find joy and meaning in simple everyday activities. For example, when your alarm goes off in the morning, instead of listening to the news or the traffic report or scrolling through social media, why not do a five-minute meditation to start your day in a positive frame of mind? Instead of just taking three deep breaths, why not also add an affirmation – 'I am enough, I know enough, I have enough' – and turn this into a loving-kindness ritual? How about using a special bowl and cup at breakfast to remind yourself to slow down and mindfully taste your food, or challenging the attitude that travelling to work is a tedious chore, and instead acknowledging the gift of meaningful work and appreciating the commute?

No matter how much you prepare for it, becoming a parent can be quite a shock. In the beginning I struggled with a destabilised sense of identity as I recovered from the wreckage of a delivery. I had to create new routines and face the fact that breastfeeding and chronic fatigue were never going to get along. The exhaustion was horrific and I had to let go of the idea of being a perfect mum. And to be honest this is something I still continually have to do, as the kids age and the landscape of the household keeps shifting. Physical exhaustion has turned into worry and mild anxiety as they enter early adulthood. All these changes invite me to alter my own routines and rituals to ensure I am showing up as the best (sometimes messy) version of myself.

The lists on the following pages are prompts to help you establish basic routines and rituals, so you can feel in control, find meaning each day, fill your tank, and give to others from a place of loving-kindness. Remember that you cannot give what you don't have, and that you need to spend some time on yourself so that you can give freely.

TURN YOUR ROUTINES
INTO RITUALS

MY INTENTIONAL RITUALS

Example List   *My List*

MORNING RITUALS	MORNING RITUALS
Wake up early, give thanks	
Take three deep breaths	
Set my intention for the day	
Make the bed	
Exercise	
Shower	
Hydrate and have a nutritious breakfast	
Take supplements	
Brush my teeth	
Allow love and kindness	

Example List	*My List*
DAYTIME FUN	**DAYTIME FUN**
Twenty-minute rest: do a guided meditation	
Write a journal entry	
Listen to a podcast	
Declutter	
Stretch my body	
Take three deep breaths every time I wash my hands	
Put some music on	
Play with a pet	
Go outside	
Catch up with a friend	
Create a mood board	

Example List	*My List*

EVENING RITUALS	EVENING RITUALS
Eat dinner and prepare tomorrow's food	
Write tomorrow's to-do list	
Touch base with a friend	
Turn my phone and devices off by 8.30 pm	
Wash my face, brush my teeth and put on essential oils	
Read ten pages of my book	
Watch TV	
Check in with myself in the mirror	
Put out clothes for tomorrow	
Take three deep breaths	
Write my gratitude journal, smile	
Choose my positive affirmation for the morning	

Once you've created your list, your go-to sheet, put it up so you can see it daily. It will guide you when you're feeling overwhelmed, and you can change it whenever you want. Play with it and see what feels best for you. Make it your creative project to research powerful morning and evening rituals. It's been said that practising rituals for twenty-one days turns them into habits.

QUICK CHECK-IN – START-OF-THE-WEEK JOURNAL PROMPT

My number-one priority is:

....

I want to do less:

....

I want to do more:

....

This week I want to feel:

....

To feel this way I will:

....

If I get stuck, I'll remember:

....

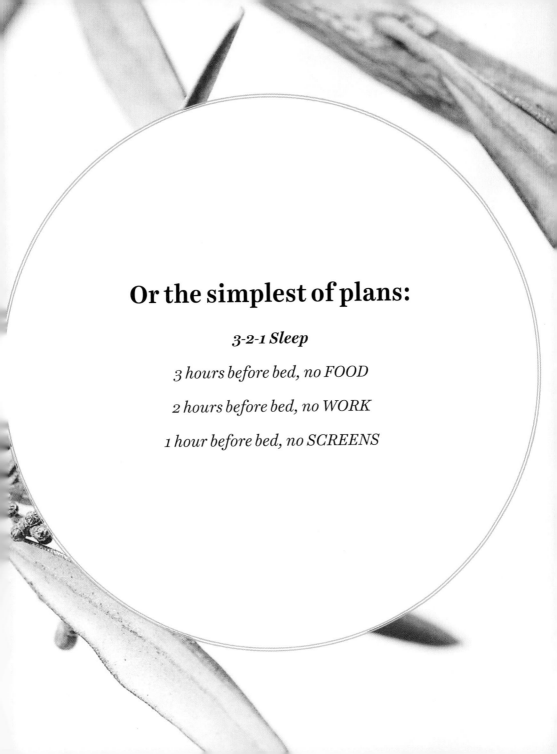

Or the simplest of plans:

3-2-1 Sleep

3 hours before bed, no FOOD

2 hours before bed, no WORK

1 hour before bed, no SCREENS

HEAL THROUGH
MINDFULNESS

Mindfulness is the ability to fully engage with whatever you are doing in the moment, free from judgement and distractions. It is a learnable skill and such an important part of your healing as you adjust to your change in circumstances.

When we took a five-month family sabbatical in the United States seven years ago, I set myself the challenge of practising mindfulness. CFS gave me the gift of learning to master the basics in life. I thought to myself, 'Where could I take myself if I focused on developing soft skills?' Mindfulness had always sounded too easy to me – I didn't have time for it, I was too busy, too driven for such things. But during that sabbatical I made it my goal to really understand it, practise it and make it a way of life. I now have a wonderful relationship with mindfulness and notice and cherish the small things: the way my dog breathes as he sleeps, the food I taste, the feeling of hot water on my skin, and so much more. My life has so much depth to it now, and I quietly appreciate all my surroundings, tapping into my five senses with incredible joy.

As well as taking time out to practise mindfulness, we can derive fulfilment from being mindful during everyday activities. Slowing our minds and focusing on the present helps us to better connect with what we are doing, tap into our inner calm, and make peace with our emotions. It highlights things we can be grateful for – things we have or are currently building – and adds dimension, tenderness and meaning to our lives, soothes our souls, and increases our sense of worth. It allows us to process the loss of what was, to let go of perfectionism, forgive and move on as we live in what is true right now. I have written a lot about mindfulness in my previous books as it is a very important self-care mindset – and it doesn't cost you anything.

For use during a panic attack, when you need to stay calm,
or anytime you feel 'disconnected' from your body.

LOOK AROUND YOU. IDENTIFY + NAME:

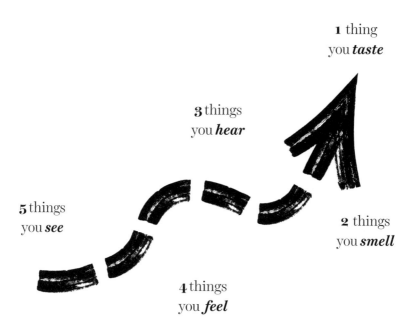

1 thing
you *taste*

3 things
you *hear*

5 things
you *see*

2 things
you *smell*

4 things
you *feel*

Feeling a little anxious or overwhelmed, or want to reconnect with yourself? Sit still and take three deep breaths.

Write five things you can see *E.g. the sun, a picture on the wall, people walking past*	
Write four things you can feel *E.g. the wind blowing, the pencil in my hand, my feet on the floor, the scarf around my neck*	
Write three things you can hear *E.g. chatter from the café, the clock ticking, birds chirping*	
Write two things you can smell *E.g. the detergent on my clothes, freshly cut grass, the smell of my tea*	
Write one thing you can taste *E.g. minty toothpaste, the lingering taste of my tea*	

The more you practise mindfulness, the more it will become a way of life. Three things to try to notice each day are what energises you, what you are grateful for and what is not working for you.

Not all storms come to disrupt your life, some come to clear your path.

Paulo Coelho

Open the Path to Positivity

As your physical and emotional reserves fill up and you begin to feel better – more stable, courageous and confident – you can start to open up to positivity and practise loving-kindness. Give yourself permission to be kind to both yourself and others, to let go a little, and to start to say yes. You will begin to find your flow again and allow some gifts to come in.

Remember that when one door closes, another door opens.

PRACTISE LOVING-KINDNESS (METTA)

Loving-kindness (metta) is the most beautiful practice. I learnt it a few years ago and it has changed me so much. It has softened me and given me something beautiful to wrap myself in when my body hurts or my mind is out of balance. The word 'metta' means unconditional loving-kindness, benevolence and goodwill. The practice, a meditation, is about making space in your heart for compassion for all living beings. You start by sending yourself some love, then someone you care about, then someone you feel neutral about, then a total stranger, then someone you dislike, then, finally, all beings. By sending peace and well-wishes to someone who may not deserve your kindness, you become stronger and help yourself to heal.

May I be happy *May you be happy*

May I be healthy *May you be healthy*

May I be safe *May you be safe*

May I live with ease *May you live with ease*

Whenever I cannot sleep, I practise this mantra and meditation. It always helps to soothe my mind. I start by sending love to myself, then to every member of my family, my suburb, my state, my country, the world, the universe. You can make up your list as you go.

I will never forget the day I was doing this meditation in a class at a health retreat and felt my whole life shift. It was like someone had turned a light on and there was no darkness or sadness anymore. I felt whole.

Put this mantra up where you can always see it, to remind yourself of its healing power. Set it as a screensaver, stick it on the mirror, or write it on a sticky note and put it on the car dashboard. This is your home base.

GIVE YOURSELF PERMISSION TO LET GO

Letting go means being willing to allow life to take you to a new and deeper place. This is not an easy thing to do. But it does not necessarily require you to completely let go of the past; compassionately allowing yourself to hold a space in your heart for it can help you to start to move forward. The process may feel messy and bumpy, but you can take your time – there is no rush – and eventually you will find your balance.

It's natural to want to hold on to the past, to the people and places we have connected with. We might choose to move on but still have trouble letting go because our job and the people we worked or lived with were a major part of our lives. We might get stuck in the bargaining stage of grief, thinking about ways things might have gone differently or better. But while we know how to fight for relationships, other people, and our job or business, sometimes they don't fight to hold on to us. And when we try to hold on to things that are letting go of us, often we only cause ourselves hurt.

THE PROCESS OF LETTING GO

» Know what's stopping you and then move it along – are they your reasons or someone else's?

» Make a decision – does this feel more bad than good? What has to change for you to feel happy? What will you gain from staying in this mindset?

» Change 'can't' to 'won't' – 'I can't' means I am giving up, while 'I won't hold on so tightly' means I am taking back some control.

» Have an anchor – be clear about why you are letting go, as you may forget in the next wave of emotion.

» Know that you are not doing something wrong; you are doing something brave, and honouring yourself.

» Don't expect to see the effects of the change immediately.

» Cry and feel it fully.

» Realise that it is okay to fall apart, pick yourself up and fall apart again – it truly is okay.

» Trust that you will be fine, because you will.

FOUR THINGS I AM WILLING TO START LETTING GO OF

1.

2.

3.

4.

If you focus on what you are afraid of, you will become paralysed by the thought of growing and evolving and will not be able to change and create a new plan. But by drawing on love, kindness and compassion, you can start to drown out fear, open yourself up to positivity, and choose to live mindfully in the present – and new opportunities will come to you. Follow your bliss, don't be afraid.

Focus on letting go, take your time, flow, and add a dash of love, kindness and compassion to the process.

FIVE THINGS YOU CAN QUIT RIGHT NOW

- » Comparing yourself to others
- » Needing other people's approval
- » Trying to please everyone
- » Putting yourself down
- » Worrying about things you can't change

START SAYING YES!

The three most important words you can say to yourself are 'Yes, I can.' 'Yes' is a beautiful word when you are ready to re-enter the world after a change.

Yes is the practice of acceptance. As we start to recover we can also start saying yes to life, open the door to positivity and allow new energy to come in.

When I had to change my business and quickly move to Plan B, I went through a period of grief. I had to take time to reconnect with myself, centre myself and heal a little. But then I started saying yes – yes to myself and to the world. New energy, new phone calls, new people and new experiences poured in, and suddenly I was writing a new book in the midst of it all.

Saying yes scares me to death half the time. It dances with my fear. If I say yes to a speaking engagement, I worry about what my client will think when they find out I have not had any speaker training. If I say yes to a dinner, I know my mind will race as I prepare to make my exit so I can go home and shut the door and feel safe again. Basic social situations are challenging for me, but funnily enough, walking into a corporate meeting, or picking up the phone to introduce myself to someone, or being interviewed on a podcast or a morning show are no problem at all. I think this is because coaching is my greatest joy, and my passion, for it overrides my nerves. It is definitely my calling, and it is a gift I received from CFS, as I never would have considered it if I hadn't worked with a life coach during my darkest days.

Saying yes doesn't mean saying yes to everything, or sacrificing or sabotaging your time, energy, values and rituals to please others. It is about giving yourself the courage and conviction to do something you know deep inside you really want to do, even if it terrifies you.

SOME REASONS WHY YOU SHOULD SAY YES

» Someone believes in you.

» You may block a miracle if you don't say yes to the opportunity.

» The opportunity may not arise again.

» Life can be fuller, richer, more creative and more vibrant when you say yes.

» It will encourage you to stretch yourself.

» By telling the world you have got this, you attract positivity.

If someone offers you an amazing opportunity to do something and you're not sure you can do it, say yes – then learn how to do it later.

Richard Branson

Don't ask yourself 'Why?', but rather 'Why not?'

THREE THINGS THAT I AM READY TO SAY YES TO:

1.

2.

3.

Remember to ask yourself, 'What is the best thing that could happen?' Think on this. How does it make you feel? Sit with it for a minute. A yes might be your only option.

FLOW AND IDENTIFY
THE GIFT

As I mentioned previously, flowing with your emotions is important. But there is a different type of flow that comes as you start to feel better. This is a time to allow yourself to move and open up again, to see where the river, the journey of life, will take you. FLOW is one of my favourite words, and I have it on my mirror and as a screensaver. It reminds me to stop holding on so tightly, to lighten up, to flow with life, other people, the world – to let go of the desire to control everything all the time. Nature is constantly showing us how to flow, so let's listen to it.

To induce a flow state, you may have to lower your expectations of both yourself and others.

THREE THINGS I CAN START TO FLOW WITH

1.

2.

3.

You may remember hearing people say, 'It was so terrible at the time, but now I see it was a gift.' Many of life's most valuable lessons come from setbacks, failures, breakdowns and major difficulties in our health, careers and relationships. There is no answer to losing a loved one, but there is an invitation to start looking for a gift that will comfort you. You may start to see that one of grief's greatest gifts is a new appreciation for the preciousness of life, and a realisation of just how important love is for yourself and for others.

This invitation is for you to find a gift. You may be ready or you may not be, but when you are ready it will be here.

Can you identify with some of these gifts?

- » I found gratitude.
- » I gained more awareness and intuition.
- » I reconnected with simple pleasures.
- » I received the gift of wisdom.
- » Grief made me a better person.
- » I have become more patient and kind.
- » I found light in the darkness.
- » I developed greater love for myself and empathy for others.
- » I learnt how to breathe.
- » I found myself.

THESE ARE SOME OF THE GIFTS I HAVE BEEN GIVEN

....

....

....

....

....

Find the gift in each day, and write it in your journal.

4. Flow
and identify
the gift

3. Start
saying yes!

2. Give
yourself
permission
to let go

1. Practise
loving-kindness
(metta)

If I cannot do great things, I can do small things in a great way.

Martin Luther
King Jr

Relinquish the Past – You've Got This

CELEBRATE THE SMALL WINS

Celebrating little wins will always help you feel more motivated. The power of progress, of small achievements, is a fundamental human need. I am my family's, friends' and clients' biggest cheerleader and always want to encourage them to celebrate small victories. They help you build momentum and confidence and allow you to feel joy. They all add up to something greater, so take notice of them, acknowledge them, give yourself a high-five, share them with a friend, and watch the universe start delivering to you.

Celebrating the little things can make the biggest difference. Contrary to what we might believe, we don't need huge wins all the time, and the thrill and satisfaction they provide often pass quickly. But it feels so good to celebrate our daily achievements: making a beautiful soup, finishing our tax return, tending to the garden, having a great work meeting, getting on the yoga mat at 6 am, or doing that task we have been avoiding. Start to pay attention to the small wins in your daily life.

During my darkest days with chronic fatigue, when I could not move, have a light on, or even find the energy to lift a finger, I remember my coach celebrating me walking to the letterbox and back. We thought it was incredible!

I knew there was a monstrously difficult journey ahead, and that I just needed to put one foot in front of the other, and that for a long time it would be a case of two steps forward, one step back – which is sometimes still the case today. The biggest challenge was working with my feelings and emotions and retraining my brain. Twenty years later these are non-negotiable daily practices, and I still celebrate all my little wins – there are many internal high-fives being had!

Every day I have a to-do list, which during the 2020 COVID-19 pandemic I called a 'joy list' to remind myself to approach each task with joy. This helped me recognise small daily achievements as I tackled the challenge of reinventing my business model.

Small wins may include waking up feeling refreshed, walking for an hour, learning something new, being complimented on the dinner you made, getting your family to work or school on time, or reaching a minor milestone you set for yourself.

LIST YOUR SMALL WINS HERE, AND PUT A STAR NEXT TO THEM, BECAUSE YOU ARE A STAR!

No matter what curve ball life throws at you, having a jar of small wins will help to keep you motivated, reassure you that you are able to pivot to Plan B, and help boost your confidence.

1 Find an empty jar.
2 Label it with a sticker or post-it note.
3 Every time you try something new or have a small win, write it down on a piece of paper and put it in the jar.

As you do this, make sure you celebrate and reflect on your progress. Alternatively, you can create a small-wins notebook or journal to record your accomplishments in, even the most minor ones. Whenever you feel unmotivated or that you are not making progress, read the notes in your jar or open up your journal to find your flow again.

Value each win. Take note of them and celebrate them. The momentum will shift, and the wins will get bigger.

Quick reflection

What progress can I celebrate?

What do I appreciate about myself?

*A year from now, I'd want my present-day
self to remember . . .*

FIND PATIENCE AND HOPE

Patience and fortitude conquer all things – **Ralph Waldo Emerson**

Patience is a virtue and a tough skill to master. I must admit it is the skill I find the hardest to develop, but also the one I most want to embrace. Patience is the ability to stay calm while waiting for an outcome that you need or want (or even for an outcome that you do not want). Impatience, on the other hand, often gives rise to frustration, and can trigger a whole range of negative emotions. Patience will help you stay calm in a pivotal moment, when things are not moving as quickly as you would like them to. Being more patient is a challenge I face on a daily basis, as I always want everything done yesterday.

TIPS TO DEVELOP YOUR PATIENCE

» **Be mindful of what is making you feel so rushed** – Your mental to-do list can become a traffic jam in your head, so write everything down on paper or on screen to decongest your thoughts.

» **Make yourself wait** – Beware of instant gratification. Waiting for things often makes us happier in the long run, so maybe wait until the weekend to watch your favourite TV show so you can really enjoy it rather than cramming it in at the end of the evening at the expense of sleep.

» **Embrace feeling uncomfortable** – Get used to this feeling, as it means you are growing and evolving. Try to avoid rushing back to your comfort zone all the time.

» **Do some deep breathing** – Slow things down and use the (literal) traffic jam or supermarket queue to practise your loving-kindness or work on your breathing, as this will ease your impatience and calm your jitters.

THINGS THAT ARE MAKING ME IMPATIENT AT THE MOMENT

1.
....

....

2.
....

....

3.
....

....

Patience is your new superpower.

Hope is like the sun, which, as we journey toward it, casts the shadow of our burden behind us.

Samuel Smiles

A single thread of hope is a very powerful thing. Hope is stronger than fear, and it is often said that where there is life there is hope. It is such a simple word, yet it means so much when you are going through a difficult time. It means the difference between hanging on and just giving up. So no matter what situation, mood or state you are in, know that you can always lean on it. Hope is allowing yourself to see light in the midst of darkness. As a coach, I am a lighthouse, shining a beam through the rough seas until the client finds their way through the storm and doesn't need me anymore. Always remember never to lose hope, as there is always tomorrow. I often tell myself this when the day didn't go well, or I didn't feel well; I just flow with it and hope that tomorrow I will feel better. There is no healing without hope.

When you're experiencing change, ask yourself, 'What if life after the change will actually be better? What if my next job is better, if my next relationship is better, if I do recover from my illness or learn to dance with it?' Hope is here for you.

SOME GENTLE REMINDERS FOR WHEN YOU FEEL HOPELESS

» Recognise your fear for what it is.

» Be softer and kinder to yourself and remember that the universe has your back.

» Seek out positivity in your life.

» Do things that give you a sense of purpose.

» Channel your energy into making a productive change.

» Give what you wish to receive. Practise saying 'yes' and be open to receiving.

» Ask for help and seek therapy if you feel you need it.

» Remember that change takes time.

WHAT DOES HOPE MEAN TO YOU AND WHAT DO YOU HOPE FOR?

Never ever lose hope.

SET SMALL TIMELINES

Setting timelines for yourself helps to get your brain into gear again and prompts you to start re-establishing goals. Since you may not be ready for big goals at this stage, as you have yet to fully pivot into a new plan, this is a great time to set small timelines – and therefore small lists – for yourself.

I love to set timelines a few different ways, and the first is by using the seasons. This allows me to feel as if I am reconnecting with the flow of nature, and really supports my mental, emotional and physical health. Seasons have the ability to influence you, to change your energy and perspective. Nature, through the seasons, shows us that change is a rule of life, and that it happens each and every day.

The seasons can prompt you to make dynamic shifts, modify your routines and set new goals. You might do different exercises, take different supplements, or establish new systems. Here is how I use the seasons to plan.

WINTER

I use this season to invite inner work, increase my supplement intake and indulge in indoor physical activities, such as yoga. I also take this time to focus on big projects, as there are fewer distractions and I don't feel as if I am missing out on any fun being had outside. I get up early and go for a walk in the icy air, then I set my goals and off I go. I write my books, do the taxes, check our insurance and finances, review my website and the back end of the business, and cook more soul-nourishing food. The fire goes on, we watch a movie or sport, and I always go to bed early.

SPRING

Spring is a transitional season. In spring, I finish the big projects I started in winter and start celebrating my wins. I start to lighten up, revive a little, take some deep breaths, enjoy the bright blue skies and watch plants sprout in the garden. I try to invite colour into my life, have some fun, try new things and reward myself for my focus and productivity during winter.

SUMMER

In summer I try not to set too many big goals outside work, and instead really enjoy life – being outdoors and watching sunsets, seeing friends and exercising. It's a time to let your hair down. This is the time I really like to let go.

AUTUMN

Autumn is one of my favourite seasons – I love the colours, the leaves and the weather, and I use it to lay the groundwork for the big goals I like to set for the winter. It is a season of preparation for me.

Write down your main focus for the upcoming season, or the small goals you want to achieve.

It's a new season. It's the perfect chance to do something new, something bold, something beautiful. Work with the seasons.

WINTER	SPRING	SUMMER	AUTUMN

Quick check-in for my journal

Last month:

The highlight of the month was . . .

This month I want to feel . . .

I will be over the moon if by the end of next month I . . .

The one pattern or habit I want to change is . . .

This month, my non-negotiable is . . .

I will nourish myself by . . .

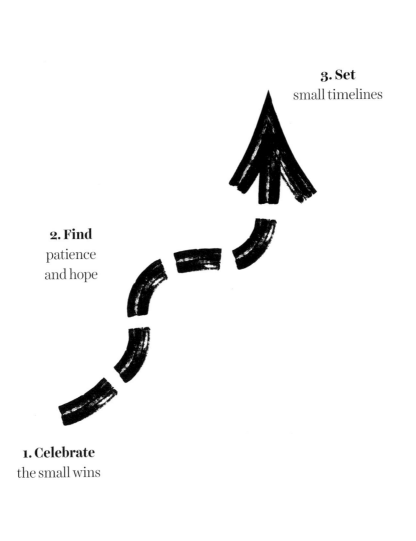

3. Set
small timelines

2. Find
patience
and hope

1. Celebrate
the small wins

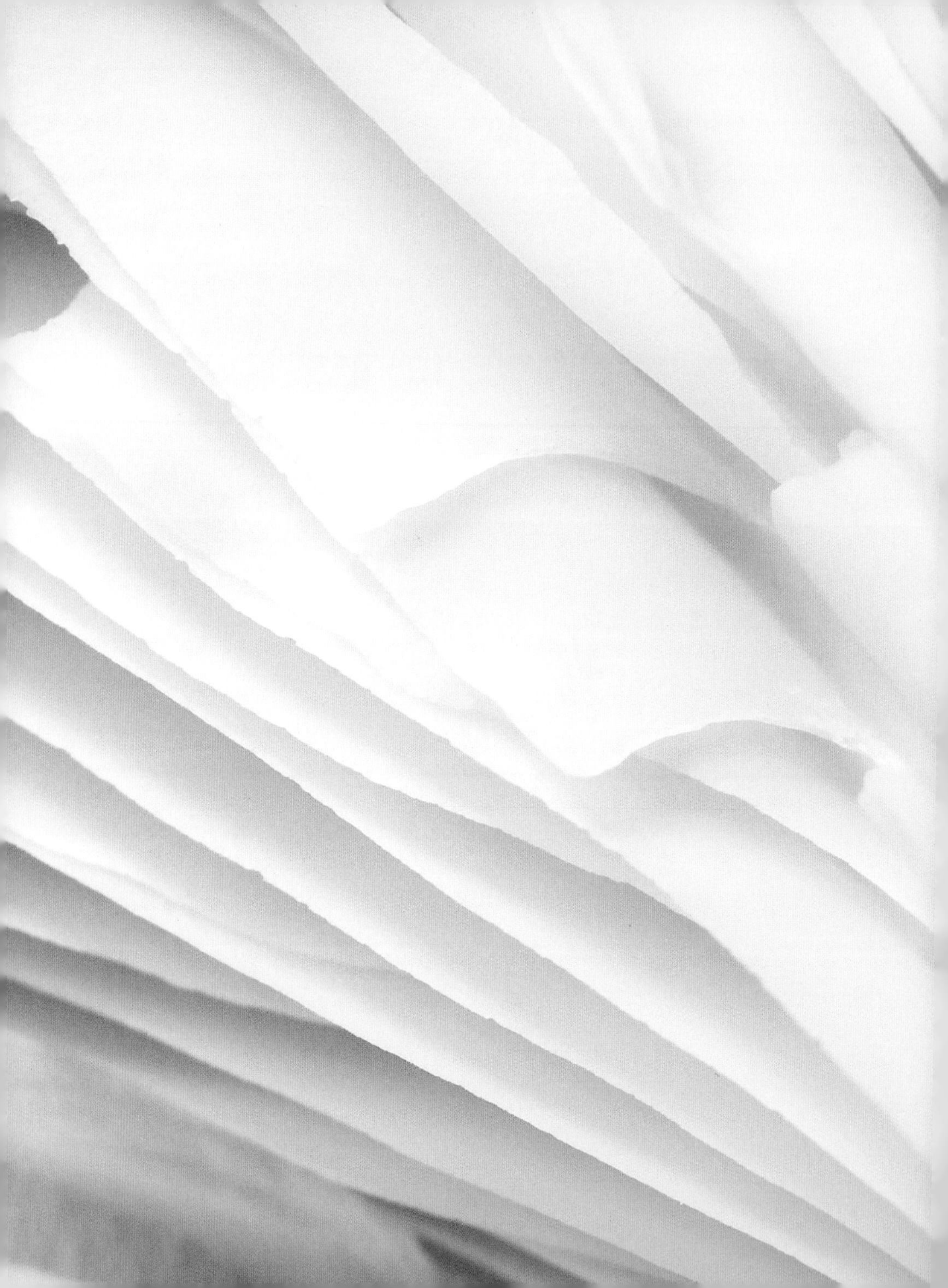

REDIRECT & RESET

Stage 3

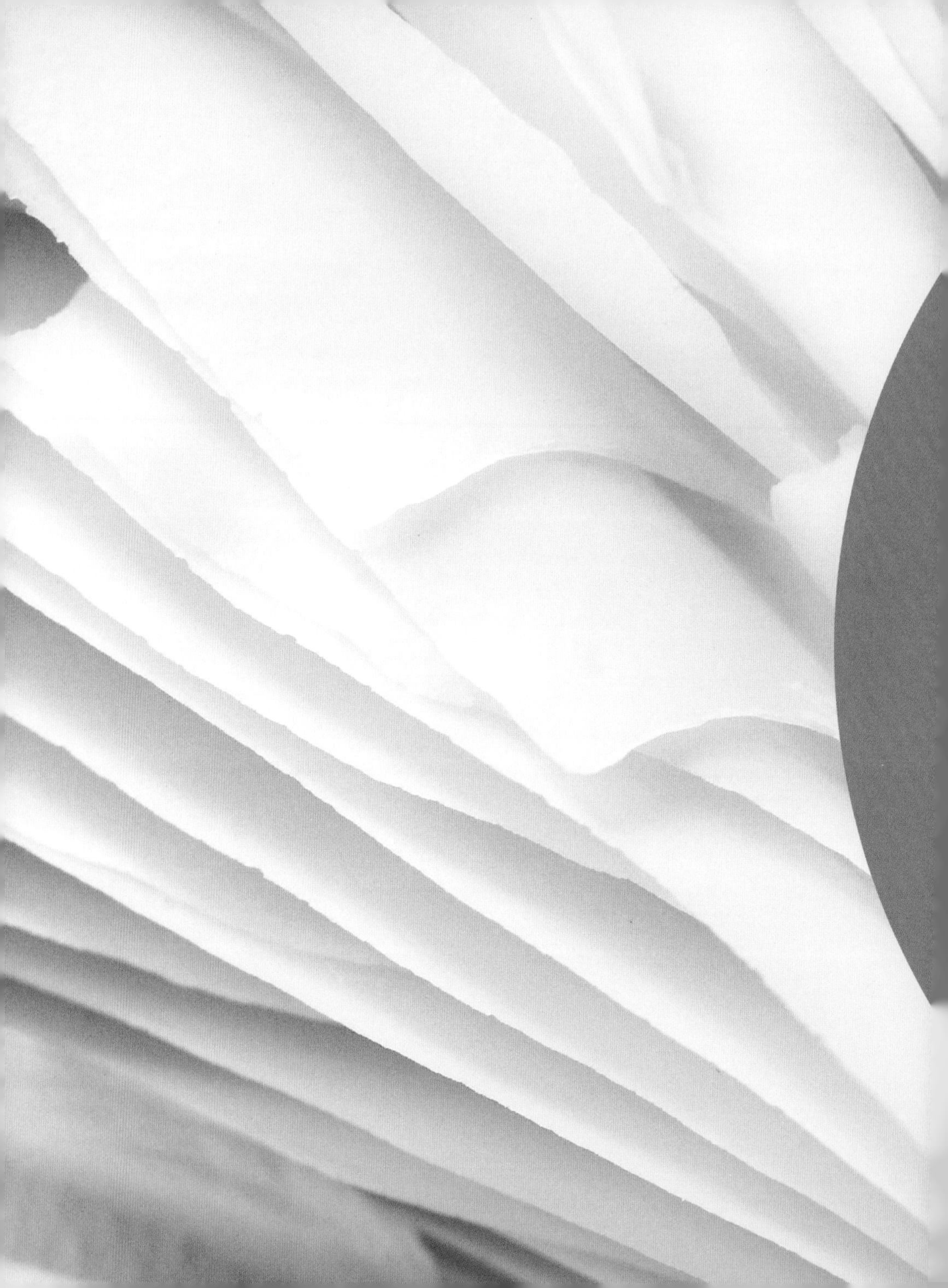

Stage 3
REDIRECT & RESET
THE PIVOT

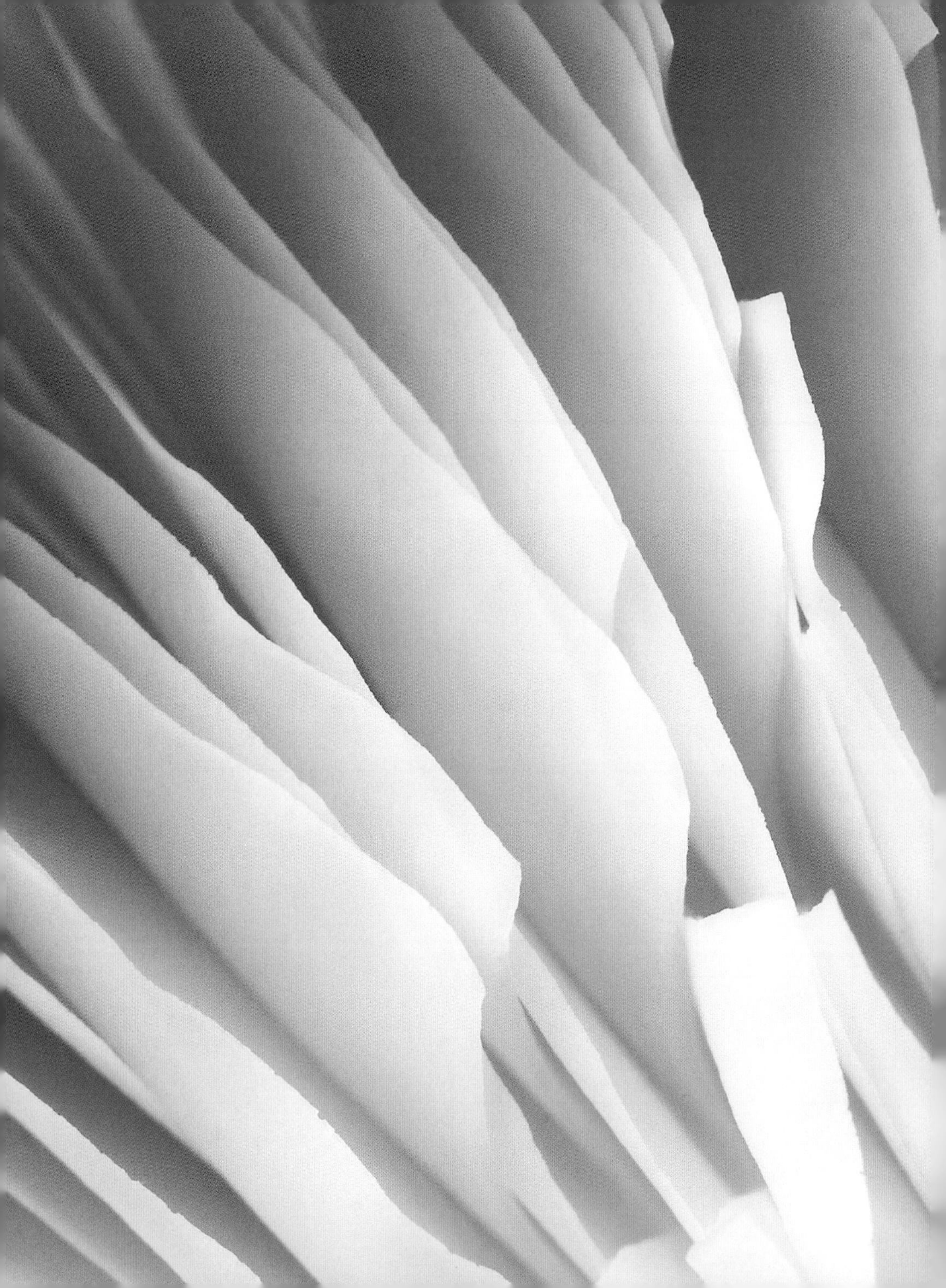

Don't ask what the world needs. Ask what makes you come alive, and go do it. Because what the world needs is people who have come alive.

———————————

Howard Thurman

The third stage of dealing with change is very exciting. It is time to come alive, to take full ownership, to explore, create and get your new self together. If you could create anything, what would it be? It can be hard to let go of your old self, your old jobs, relationships and friendships – to start to unlearn, gently let go and forgive – but I fully believe in you. I back you. This is your time.

Creating Plan B is not about hitting the reset button on life. We don't wipe the hard drive clean of all of our memories. This is about changing direction and it is a twofold process. You must admit to what is not working and then you must be willing to adopt a new mindset and try new things.

I will guide you to become a student again, a student of life, growth, self-care and authenticity. Your Plan B starts right here and will be a true articulation of who you are, as you have attained new wisdom by doing the work on yourself, sitting in silence and taking the breaths, and can now build hardiness and resilience and find meaning in what has happened.

Let's create a new mindset and develop a new plan, a new wholehearted vision for your future. Let's work together to fire up your determination to turn the change, loss and suffering you have experienced into something good. You are not broken – you are just rebuilding your foundation and reforming yourself. This is your opportunity for a fresh start, a more meaningful life, where you get to choose courage over comfort. So let's hit the empowerment button.

At the heart of a pivot is personal growth and the mindset of being open to who you want to become.

4. Ignite your flame
Choose your cheer squad
Practise visualisation
Be the change you wish to see

2. Plant new seeds
Challenge your comfort zone
Train your brain
Set boundaries

3. Create your road map
Simplify your life
Write your new vision
Set fresh goals

1. Rebuild your foundation
Redefine your values and purpose
Clarify what you want
Upgrade your attitude

Rebuild Your Foundation

Whatever it takes, feel the fear and do it anyway. You can choose freedom over fear. You will create a fulfilling life when you accept that loss, change, failures and challenges are a part of life. You can minimise your fear and increase your empowering thoughts by monitoring your self-talk, taking steps forward and taking action. By taking some small – or even large but considered – risks, you can build your resilience and develop more grit. You have done the healing and put the necessary time into yourself, and can now begin to trust and love yourself enough to start saying yes to opportunities. I believe in you. You can transform fear into faith.

Values are like fingerprints. Nobody's are the same, but you leave 'em all over everything you do.

Elvis Presley

REDEFINE YOUR VALUES AND PURPOSE

If you have read my book *The Life Plan*, you will know that my values are central to my life, and that I prioritise them above all else, including my career. Our values help us find our purpose and are the gateway to our authentic selves; they are our starting point, the core of our emotional intelligence and our number-one decision-making tool.

Identifying values is the first exercise I do with every client, as we cannot plan or create when we are not clear on what is in our soul, what is most important to us. Our goals and sense of purpose are grounded in our values. They are our compass through life, and are shaped by everything that has happened to us and those who have influenced us, including our upbringing, education, family, friends and peers. So take a moment now to consider your values and reaffirm the essence of who you are.

FAMILY HAPPINESS Quality time, bonding	**SELF-RESPECT** Sense of personal identity, pride	**GENEROSITY** Helping others, improving society
COMPETITIVENESS Winning, taking risks	**RECOGNITION** Acknowledgement, status	**WISDOM** Discovering and understanding knowledge
FRIENDSHIP Close relationships with others	**ADVANCEMENT** Promotions	**SPIRITUALITY** Strong religious or spiritual beliefs
AFFECTION Love, caring	**HEALTH** Mental, physical	**LOYALTY** Devotion, trustworthiness
COOPERATION Working well with others, teamwork	**RESPONSIBILITY** Being accountable for results	**CULTURE** Traditions, customs, beliefs
ADVENTURE New challenges	**FAME** Public recognition	**INNER HARMONY** Being at peace
ACHIEVEMENT A sense of accomplishment	**INVOLVEMENT** Belonging, being involved with others	**ORDER** Stability, conformity, tranquility
WEALTH Getting rich, making money	**ECONOMIC SECURITY** Strong and consistent income streams	**CREATIVITY** Being imaginative, innovative
ENERGY Vitality, vigour	**PLEASURE** Fun, laughter, a leisurely lifestyle	**INTEGRITY** Honesty, sincerity, standing up for oneself
FREEDOM Independence, autonomy	**POWER** Control, authority or influence over others	**PERSONAL DEVELOPMENT** Use of personal potential

Choose your top three values from this list and write them here, and next to these values write why they are so important to you. What do they mean to you?

MY TOP THREE VALUES

1.

2.

3.

THESE ARE THE VALUES I WORK FOR ON A DAILY BASIS:

HEALTH – Mental, emotional, physical and spiritual. Health is my most important value and I do activities each day to support all four pillars of health.

RELATIONSHIPS – I want to show up and be the best version of myself for my family, friends and clients, so I need to ensure my schedule is designed so I have space to refuel and top up my tank in order to be this person.

ACHIEVEMENT – I am so happy on days when I feel a sense of achievement. To create that spark I commit to making a to-do list – a joy list – every day and ticking it off. My mini self-care moments are the hardest achievements but the most important for my health and the longevity of my career, so they need to be on my joy list.

Your values will keep your world in alignment and serve as your foundation as you shift to Plan B. They will keep your mind decluttered, give you confidence and guide you when you need to take a risk. When you are making a decision, always ask yourself, 'Does this serve my values?'

I see my values daily as they are on the mirror, in my diary and set as my screensaver. During lockdown, when I needed to turn my mindset around, I put my values on a sticky note on my laptop. I always want them to be visible, to be 'in my face', to remind me of what is really important and to guide me in my actions and decisions. They spur me on and ground me. Working for my values has served me for the past twenty years and allowed me to live a great life in spite of my health conditions and all the little ruts I have found myself in.

Your values also help you to investigate your purpose, which is simply what propels you to move forward – your 'why?' Why am I writing this book? Because I hope to help people, one by one, to manage and feel supported when major change has happened to them or they have decided to make a major change. Not many people like the feeling of change – it often comes with fear – but I hope this book will allow people to kick fear aside and choose freedom, energy, life and joy.

Writing this book served my values and was a judgement-free process. I told myself I could never do it. I find writing hard but I am feeling the fear and doing it anyway. I decided that I just had to trust my instincts and write this book for myself, as I go through change, and for you, the reader, wherever you may be on your journey. I am talking to you one on one, and not to some big imaginary audience. I am writing to you the way I coach.

I am also writing Plan B's for myself, because like everyone's, my Plan A's do not always work out. I work through every stage of this book, sometimes on a monthly basis. What I am sharing with you is how I actually live my life, constantly adapting my plans to my present situation – my health, relationships, work and the ever-changing world around me – and adapting where required. We are in this together.

SOME PROMPTS TO HELP YOU RECONNECT WITH YOURSELF

- » What makes you happy?
- » Where do you most enjoy spending time?
- » If money was no issue, how would you spend your time?
- » What do you do easily and effortlessly?
- » What are you doing when you feel alive?
- » What do you want your life to look like?
- » What do you want to leave behind and what do you want to take with you?
- » What do you want to give to others or to the world?

Asking yourself these questions will help you start to find your passion, live with daily purpose and find your spark once again. Put your values where you can see them daily. They are what you work for.

Make peace with the mirror and watch your reflection change.

Anon

CLARIFY WHAT YOU WANT

To know what you want, you need to listen to your heart, reconnect with yourself, and tap into your inner voice, as that is where all the answers are.

When you were a child, how close did you stand to the mirror? If you observe a three- or four-year-old, you will see that they stand right up close, staring, smiling, pulling faces, dancing and even kissing the mirror as they fully embrace and accept the person staring back at them. That person is their best friend. When did you last look in the mirror and acknowledge your best friend, the one who was there when you took your first breath and who will be there when you take your last? When did you last check in to see how they are?

Learning to love yourself is a prerequisite for attracting joy in your life. You will have heard many times that you cannot give love if you don't have it. So I invite you to walk to the mirror and reconnect with your best friend. It may feel awkward, silly or embarrassing to start with, and you will need to look past the wrinkles, the supposed 'faults' you may see on the outside, but with practice you will feel a big internal shift occur. You will start to develop a deeper, more meaningful relationship with yourself. You will stop seeing drama, overwhelm and fear and instead start to hear the voices of your inner child and your older, wiser self. Listen. What are they telling you to do?

I do this exercise daily, which might sound strange, but it is just so lovely to be at peace with myself and to listen to the voices I have just described – they speak all the time and it is great to have them with me. My coach made me try this exercise when I was in the depths of CFS and could barely function. Instead of hating myself for having it, I had to make peace with it so I could set some goals and move forward. Today I still need to make peace with it, so every day I address the mirror.

Look in the mirror and replace self-criticism with self-love and care. Say hello with kindness and openness every time you brush your teeth and wash your hands or face – look up and speak to yourself like you would to your best friend.

WHAT IS MY OLDER, WISER SELF TELLING ME TO DO RIGHT NOW?

1.

2.

3.

Look at yourself in the mirror and don't be afraid to notice how beautiful you are.

Yoko Ono

Ben, a client of mine, was an Olympic coach who for many years put his heart and soul into his job. The athlete he trained won a lot of international events but never got onto the podium at the Olympics. After all those years, all that time, energy, dedication and effort, they never got the prize they were after. It took Ben a long time to get over this, to deal with and move on from the deep disappointment, and to adopt the attitude that not everything goes the way you want it to.

In the same year that the athlete passed away in a freak accident, Ben also lost his wife to postnatal depression. His healing was based on seeing his daughter as a gift from his wife, choosing a place in his heart where his wife would forever be with him, and being grateful for the time they had together. He chose to heal from the death of the athlete by preserving cherished memories of all the time they had spent on the road, all their ups and downs, and making an effort to incorporate the athlete's best qualities into his own personality. He healed by looking in the mirror, by seeing a new chapter opening as the old one was closing, by choosing to see a huge number of options as he lifted his head up and looked at his reflection. He saw his older self saying, 'You've got this, keep moving forward, create a new plan.' He looked after himself more, journalled every night, kept his phone out of his bedroom, and started reading again. The book in which he chose to write his values became his guide, and he wrote down reflections daily, wrote about his daughter and his new ambitions, and this gave him clarity and put him in a better place each day. He saw how much choice he had to move forward.

So become best friends with yourself, listen to your wisdom, and ask yourself, 'What is my eighty-year-old self telling me to do today? Slow down, go for it, be kind, be daring, you've got this, it is time, you can't fail, it's okay, be happy?'

Now let's ask the question – what do you really want? I always ask my clients this question twice, and the answers are always different. First express what you want, and then ask yourself again – and this time go deeper – 'What do I really want?'

The most powerful questions to ask yourself each day are 'What do I really want?' and 'What do I need to change right now?'

WHAT DO I WANT?

....

....

....

....

WHAT DO I REALLY WANT?

....

....

....

....

Your attitude, not your aptitude, will determine your altitude.

Zig Ziglar

UPGRADE YOUR
ATTITUDE

Your attitude is your altitude. What you think about yourself and your future prospects will determine your level of success.

A positive attitude will lead you to happier days. Your attitude is your driving force – it will either pull you up or drag you down. I am sure you have been around someone with a bad, toxic or pessimistic attitude. How did it make you feel? Did it light you up? Probably not. So my question to you is this: What attitude do you have, and what are you giving to others? I invite you to look on the bright side. What if things can be better than they were before? What if you can do this? What if you allow yourself to meet new people and try new things? When injected with positivity, your attitude will deliver more joy, energy and success than one that lacks this vibrancy.

I had to change my attitude towards my health and view it not as a hindrance but as a gift. I have had to reset my life and accept new circumstances many times. When the best-laid plans go awry, when the world changes and all your plans change with it, you can choose not to be the victim.

Embrace your confident self. Imagine how you would look, walk, talk and behave if you were the best version of yourself. Challenge your inner critic, the people-pleasing and perfectionist part of your-self, and move towards the part that is an adventurer, a warrior, a dreamer and a storyteller.

Life is 10% what happens to you and 90% how you react to it.

Charles Swindoll

WAYS TO CHANGE YOUR ATTITUDE

- » Believe you are able to change.

- » Start your day with a positive attitude.

- » Develop an attitude of gratitude.

- » Look to positive role models.

- » Turn your to-do list into your joy list.

- » Look for the good in others.

- » Let go of resentment.

- » Choose your company wisely – spend more time with positive people.

- » Take action and then let go as you wait to see the results.

- » Stop and challenge negative internal dialogue and instead try to think positively.

- » Find more pleasure in the simple things in life.

- » Give yourself permission to receive.

- » Think about how your attitude will help you in life.

THREE WAYS I CAN CHANGE MY ATTITUDE

1.

2.

3.

Remember that your mind is like a parachute; it will work better when it is open. If you make a daily effort to move towards a 'yes I can' attitude, you will be rewarded. You have the ability to change.

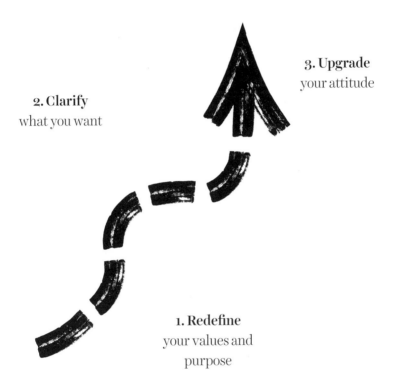

3. Upgrade
your attitude

2. Clarify
what you want

1. Redefine
your values and
purpose

Do one thing every day that scares you.

Mary Schmich

Plant New Seeds

CHALLENGE YOUR COMFORT ZONE

This is the time to stretch out of your comfort zone. A comfort zone is a beautiful place to be, but remember that nothing grows in there. So embrace 'getting comfortable with feeling uncomfortable'. I have the previous sentence up on my mirror. Trying to stop a habit – for example, making sure you have five alcohol-free days a week – is uncomfortable for many, as is learning a new skill, as many of us had to do at the beginning of 2020, when we were forced to become familiar with programs such as Zoom, Webex and Microsoft Teams. Using them was challenging and stressful at first, but now it is easy and effortless. Imagine if we allowed ourselves opportunities to grow and try new things without waiting for them to be forced upon us.

When my mind or body feel stuck, my challenge is to create movement. To go out. To see people. To scare myself a little. To dance with fear and see what is on the other side. To move gently, not aggressively, to slowly keep growing and working on myself, to encourage myself as I would a best friend or client.

Just as ships are not designed to sit in the harbour, as the famous saying goes, neither are you designed to sit and do nothing. You are designed to sail the wide open seas, to push your boundaries, to unlock your dormant potential and discover what you are capable of if you only step outside your comfort zone. A comfort zone is a safe place between growth spurts, but it becomes stagnant if you stay there for too long. My job as a coach is to hold your hand as you emerge from your comfort zone. That is how we get results. Remember that courage is contagious!

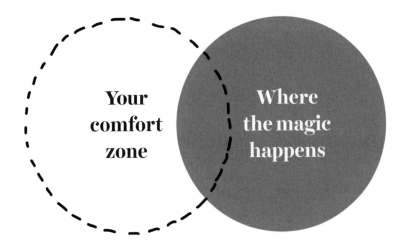

Your comfort zone

Where the magic happens

SOME SMALL BUT POWERFUL STEPS YOU CAN TAKE TO GET GOING

» Take a different route home – switch up your routine.

» Take the first step – remember that the first day at the gym is the worst.

» Say yes more often – even if you are not quite ready.

» Put yourself in a new environment – try a new restaurant in a different suburb.

» Stop procrastinating – make a decision now and just do it!

» Dare to ask – just ask and see what happens.

» Distance yourself from people and situations that do not align with your values and positive mindset.

» Rationalise your fear – if it is safe to do so, you can push through it.

» Do what you are afraid of – tell yourself you are fearless.

» Give up some of your control – allow others to lead sometimes.

» Ask questions other people don't like to – be real, be authentic, speak from your heart and not your ego.

»   Physically embody change – practise the power stance and pose like Wonder Woman or Superman.

»   Make it a habit to try something new – if it feels a little good, keep going and it will become great.

»   Reflect on your greatest accomplishments – how did you take the first step?

»   Keep a list of growth goals – practise public speaking, take a risk.

»   Remember that tomorrow is a new day – take the chance – the odds are better than you think – and forget about being perfect.

I WILL CHALLENGE MYSELF BY DOING THE FOLLOWING THINGS:

1.

2.

3.

4.

You can do this. Remember to get comfortable with feeling uncomfortable, as this means you are growing and evolving. You may not feel 100 per cent confident, but just go for it. Magic happens outside your comfort zone. If you fail, quit quickly, fail fast and try again.

TRAIN YOUR BRAIN

Whatever we plant in our subconscious mind and nourish
with repetition and emotion will one day become a reality
– Earl Nightingale

What we think shapes how we feel. Regardless of whether we are naturally a 'glass half full' or a 'glass half empty' person, we can boost our mental health and wellbeing and our energy levels by reaffirming what we want and how we want to feel.

I am constantly training my brain; I see it as a computer. I know that if I do not activate the right programs each morning, viruses will come and shut everything down. So I affirm that I am strong, safe and healthy, I can do this, I welcome change, I am open to receiving. For so long I have just given and not been open to receiving. I used to find it hard to take a compliment, or celebrate my birthday, or make any sort of fuss at all with regard to myself. I have really had to work hard to train my brain to be open, to celebrate, to feel, to receive, and to give others the gift of giving to me. A friend once said to me, 'Don't be selfish, please have a birthday dinner, we want to go out and celebrate you, so please don't stop us and squash our joy.' I still struggle with receiving, but thanks to affirmations I am a lot more open to it now, and it will be forever in my practice.

Affirmations, or mantras, are personal and express a belief that you want to embrace and claim as your own. Constantly repeating them helps your brain to form new thought patterns. Athletes are great at practising this sort of thinking – they do not turn up to events believing they will lose, but rather train their brain to send signals to their body that they can do it, they can win. Training the brain is like going to the gym for the mind; neuroscience has proven that the more we 'work out' our neural pathways, the stronger they become.

Ella is a partner in an established law firm and wanted to intro-duce a new level of care for the mental health and wellbeing of staff. During this period of transition we constantly worked on the phrase 'let it be joyful, easy and effortless'. My challenge was for her to lean in to the process, to dance with it, to not be disheartened by obsta-cles but to keep chipping away. She introduced me to the company by bringing me in to speak to the staff, after which I ran virtual live coaching sessions focused on mental health and wellbeing coping strategies, and she was chosen to be part of a panel that enabled her to start actively introducing changes. In her call to me she said, 'I wanted this but what if I am not good enough, what if I don't speak well enough, what if I haven't prepared properly due to my huge work-load at the moment?' Immediately we went to her values, and worked on the affirmations 'I am enough', 'I know enough', 'let this be a joyful experience' and 'what if it turns out to be easy and effortless?' She just needed to train her brain to flow: on the other side of fear, greatness was waiting to greet her.

I am sure you have heard the phrase 'you are what you think', so take a moment to check in with your thoughts. What are you thinking about – failure or success? Self-sabotage or self-care? Affirmations, as we've discussed, are positive words repeated often. And although we cannot rely purely on words to achieve success and feel great, we need to take these newly programmed thoughts and turn them into actions in order to achieve our goals and dreams. They are a great foundation for our new plan, a simple way to start changing our system.

MAKE POSITIVE THINKING A NEW HABIT BY USING AFFIRMATIONS TO RETRAIN YOUR BRAIN

1 Make them resonate with you personally.

2 Use present tense – not 'I want to be joyful' but 'I am joyful'.

3 Put them on repeat – I write mine in my journal each day.

EXAMPLE AFFIRMATIONS YOU CAN WRITE IN YOUR JOURNAL, PUT ON YOUR MIRROR OR SET AS A SCREENSAVER

» I am worthy, I am open, I have everything I need.

» Today is easy and effortless.

» I love myself and accept myself exactly as I am.

» I am living life to the fullest today.

» I am brave and stand up for myself.

» Today I will replace my old habits with more positive ones.

» The perfect partner for me will come into my life.

» I radiate joy and kindness.

» This too shall pass.

» I am willing to step outside my comfort zone; I am letting go of fear.

» I am defeating my illness each day.

» I am at peace with the world.

» My life is just beginning.

You can create your own affirmations based on your needs and wants, and they will form the foundation for you to take action as you leave your comfort zone. Write them down, say them with conviction and make them happen.

MY TWO FAVOURITE AFFIRMATIONS TODAY ARE:

1.

....

....

....

2.

....

....

....

Write your affirmations out daily, learn them and memorise them, and then you will be ready for action.

I have the
freedom
and power
to create
the life
I desire.

SET BOUNDARIES

Boundaries are non-negotiable for me; without them, I burn out and collapse. This means I sometimes have to say no to myself, to others and to events. Setting boundaries is an important part of your mental health and wellbeing, as without them you may find yourself experiencing poor relationships, anger, resentment, stress, financial burdens, wasted time, profound exhaustion and burnout. Boundaries can be physical or emotional, loose or rigid, with the most supportive boundaries falling somewhere between the latter two.

I often help people to set boundaries around their career so they have room for a better personal life. This makes them more connected to their friends and family, which in turn makes them happier and gives them greater fulfilment and more longevity in their career.

Emily, who I coached many years ago, had no boundaries with anyone. She would work whenever she was asked to and do everything for everyone whenever requested to. She was a real people-pleaser and had no regard for herself or her time, which left her depleted and often resentful and deepened her sense of worthlessness. What would happen if she said the occasional no? If she allowed herself to receive and not just give? As she restored her balance her life opened up and she began to honour herself. After her marriage ended she healed and set new boundaries for herself, and I am pleased to say she can now receive, has the most beautiful new husband and life, and is the healthiest she has ever been.

Boundaries exist to protect you. It is no use starting to grow some beautiful grass if you let everyone walk or drive all over it. Protect your energy, your time, your emotions, your dreams, your finances and your self-esteem.

HOW TO IMPLEMENT BOUNDARIES

DEFINE - Identify the desired boundary.

COMMUNICATE - Say what you need.

KEEP IT SIMPLE - Don't over-explain, just say why the boundary is important.

SET CONSEQUENCES - Hold yourself and others accountable if the boundary is crossed.

The best boundaries are based on your core values. Here are some areas in which to set healthy boundaries so you can feel confident and supported.

» **Food and drink** – Alcohol-free days, no coffee after midday if it affects your sleep, less refined sugar.

» **Sleep** – Go to bed by 10 pm (unless at a function) so you can get up at 6 am.

» **Finances** – Put your own financial needs before others' and set a spending limit to protect your savings.

» **Technology** – Set a 9 pm tech curfew. No phone in the bedroom.

» **Work** – Set a 'tools down' time; you are a human being.

» **Friends and family** – Allow yourself to say an empowered 'no' sometimes, or tell them you only have an hour.

» **Partner** – Clearly communicate your basic expectations.

MY NEW BOUNDARIES TO EXPLORE ARE:

....

....

....

....

....

....

You need to protect yourself, your energy and your emotions so you can shine brightly.

Daring to set boundaries is about having the courage to love ourselves, even when we risk disappointing others.

Brené Brown

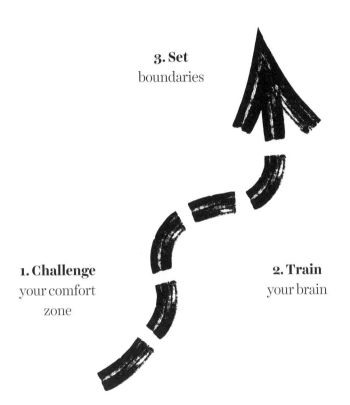

3. Set
boundaries

1. Challenge
your comfort
zone

2. Train
your brain

Create Your Road Map

Whether you, your circumstances or the world has changed, it is never too late to create your Plan B. The beauty of this is that you can do it over and over again.

Know where you are going, what direction you want to head in, and take one step at a time.

WORDS THAT MAY INSPIRE YOU

- » Peace of mind
- » New friends
- » Treasured intimacy
- » Free time
- » Freedom to travel
- » Daily exercise
- » Healthy eating
- » Space and independence
- » Strength and confidence
- » Exploration
- » Creative writing
- » New hobbies
- » Self-expression

SIMPLIFY YOUR LIFE

I invite you to quickly declutter so you have space in your life for new opportunities to come in. To live simply and not overcomplicate things is the ultimate sophistication.

ASK YOURSELF THESE TWO POWERFUL QUESTIONS
Do I need this?
Or: Do I want this?
(In other words: Do I actually require it?)

I ask myself these questions a lot. They help me to not get caught up in the game of keeping up with the Joneses on social media. They allow me to clean out my home regularly, to do a sweep of my life and keep it simple. This doesn't mean I never buy anything I want, but it does mean that I check first to see if the purchase will give me fulfilment. I consciously avoid buying small, unnecessary objects that may provide a flash of joy but end up cluttering my life and home. I keep thinking of the word 'stuffocation', and ask myself, 'Do I really want this?' This means I can channel my discretionary income into investing in things that make my heart soar, such as travelling with my family and exploring new places. I invest in experiences rather than things.

I regularly work on my finances, relationships, friendships, habits, health and wellbeing and make an effort to keep simplifying and streamlining my life. I now see having an attitude of simplicity as a great strength as it reduces a lot of unnecessary stress and drama.

Ella, the lawyer I mentioned earlier, was completely overwhelmed when I met her. She had just made partner at her law firm, and as soon as I said, 'Let's just simplify it all,' I could see the pressure valve open and let out the stress. We started small and slowly decluttered her health, her thoughts, her home and her life.

In my book *The Life Plan* there are charts and checklists for decluttering each area of your life. But here are some quick fixes to begin with:

- » Set three key goals for the day and focus on achieving them.

- » Declutter one room in your house at a time and do it thoroughly.

- » Donate old books that no longer serve you to make way for new inspiration.

- » Plan your schedule at least a few weeks in advance, and factor in time for exercise and self-care activities that cater to your four pillars of health (see page 108).

» Pre-prepare your weekday meals and snacks.

» Journal every night before bed to offload your thoughts.

And whether you are doing things for yourself, your family, your friends, your colleagues, your career or your finances, ask yourself, 'Is there a simpler way I can do this?'

THINGS IN MY LIFE I NEED TO SIMPLIFY RIGHT NOW

1.

2.

3.

4.

WRITE YOUR NEW VISION

THE JOURNEY OF A THOUSAND MILES BEGINS WITH A VISION

Plan B is sometimes thought of as a completely different plan or approach. But in the startup world, as in this book, it is often referred to as a pivot – something that may require a whole new map or may just require you to tweak your vision. Take your time to get clear about where you are right now and where you want to go; only then can you plot your path. The creation of a new or altered pathway needs to start with a vision, with an end in sight.

So open your mind, be bold, be daring, think big instead of small, focus on success, infuse your plans with passion, and don't worry about exactly how things might unfold.

Penny, one of my clients, lost her husband in a lightning strike. As farmers, they had regularly discussed Plan B – what they would do if something happened to one of them, of course never thinking anything would. Penny expressed to me that because they'd had these conversations, when her life changed and her worst fear actually came true, she felt a glimmer of comfort in the knowledge that they had a plan. She had something to work with that they had worked on together.

Our vision for the future is like a road map. We may have to deviate from our planned route here and there, but we will still know where we are headed.

I change my plans and adapt all the time, but it feels great to have a base plan.

Don't look back – you're not going that way.

Mary Engelbreit

SOME THOUGHT-STARTERS

How old will you be in one, three and five years' time?

What are your values?

What is most important to you?

Who inspires you and why?

Who are your role models and mentors?

What life experiences do you want to have?

What does economic security mean to you?

How fit, strong and flexible do you want to be?

What hobbies do you want to take up?

Where do you want to travel?

What makes you smile or brings you sheer delight?

Whose permission do you need to start taking responsibility?

What kind of work do you want to be doing?

What do you need to do for your mental and emotional health?

Who brings you joy?

What do you want to learn?

What will your passion project be?

Where do you want to live?

What do you really want for your future?

Set a vision that inspires, excites and scares you at the same time. Don't be afraid to go where you've never been and to do what you've never done, because both are necessary if you want to have what you've never had and be who you've never been. Plot all of your thoughts, then sit back, look at your plan and allow it to inspire you!

MY VALUES ARE:

....

....

....

....

MY VISIONS ARE:

....

....

....

	One year from now. Age:	Three years from now. Age:	Five years from now. Age:	What can I do today?
PERSONAL				
FAMILY				
HOME				
FINANCES				
FRIENDS/ SOCIAL				
CAREER				
HOBBIES				
BUCKET LIST				

THE POWER OF THE VISION BOARD

I love vision boards (I have several!) and redo them every three years. They give me great joy. Even if I don't achieve everything I want to, they appeal to my best self, and I make better decisions because of them. My favourite picture on my vision board is of an old Greek tomato farmer, full of wrinkles, no teeth, laughing. He reminds me not to take life so seriously all the time, to lighten up, find some joy and not get too stuck in the stormy seas.

1 THEY GIVE ENERGY

Where your focus goes, your energy flows. The pictures, words, quotes, affirmations and goals on your vision board spark new interest and energy and help you to focus on bringing your dreams to life.

2 THEY GIVE INSPIRATION

Each and every item you add to your vision board must spark emotions in you. The feelings generated by these items will come true if you allow them to. This will make your vision board more meaningful and motivating rather than just decorative.

3 THEY GIVE MOTIVATION

Visualisation is one of the most popular, effective and motivating mind workouts you can do. As discussed earlier, Olympic athletes have been using this tool for decades – tuning in to images of success on a daily basis – to improve their performance and stay energised and on track.

Make a vision board to inspire yourself daily and to support your decision-making processes. Live your dream to whatever extent you can with every action, task, conversation, interaction, purchase and decision.

Head to www.shannahkennedy.com to create your vision board by downloading the free printable vision board kit.

Extra activity – script a day of your future life as if it is your present life. Write about your future life as if your vision has already been realised.

Setting goals is the first step in turning the invisible into the visible.

Tony Robbins

SET FRESH GOALS

You lay the path to achieving your vision by setting new goals. Breaking your plan down into bite-size goals allows you to keep it simple, build momentum and boost your confidence. Each goal moves you towards your vision. Set them almost out of reach, to stretch your-self a little. I also suggest including two tasks you have been putting off; for example, starting a new fitness plan, doing your tax return or a visit to the dentist. Ticking these tasks off your list will help to create the momentum you need.

I admit I am addicted to goals – I just love them and they give me energy. I set small ones – a goal of the day, and so on – so I feel like I am moving in the right direction. Often my goals are to do something, create something, do more work, but sometimes they are simply to sit still and switch off, to find the silence so that clarity comes in. Some-times the biggest goal of all is to do something that nourishes my soul and fills my energy tank, such as cuddling or taking some small time-outs to just play with Rex, my dog, which I have realised really improves my physical and mental wellbeing.

In March 2020, when the global COVID-19 pandemic hit, my speaking business collapsed in one week, as all my conferences and travel plans had to be cancelled for the rest of the year. By being gentle with myself, acknowledging and accepting the situation, I returned to the basics: my values, and reconnecting with myself in the mirror, to get away from all the breaking news, and the fear that was triggered by such an enormous and overwhelming change. I quickly turned to setting new goals, focusing on what I could control and not wasting energy on what I couldn't.

MY NEW GOALS WERE SIMPLE AND EFFECTIVE

SELF: To park my disappointment and let it go. I had to look in the mirror each morning and set my intention for the day, and be gentle with myself as waves of overwhelm, anxiety, joy, happiness, sadness and fear rolled in and out – there were so many emotions running through me at the start of the pandemic. I had to go back to the basic foundation of my health and set daily goals such as moving my body for an hour, eating wholefoods, drinking one litre of water, meditating in silence for at least fifteen minutes to process my thoughts and find stillness, sleeping at a regular time – from 10 pm to 6 am – choosing an attitude of gratitude, and fully supporting my family, friends and clients in any way I could. Once I had these foundational goals, I could then set smaller goals and write them on sticky notes on my desk. I cleaned the house – every single cupboard – did my taxes and finances, and saw a financial planner and got very clear on where I wanted to get to. We also decided to renovate parts of our house, given that all our holiday plans had been cancelled.

CAREER: I had to try to re-embrace myself, to adjust to working all alone again. I mourned no longer being part of a business duo, The Essentialists, with Lyndall Mitchell. At times I would sit in incredible grief and sadness, knowing we would not be doing the work that gave us both the greatest joy for at least another two years. I started coaching full-time online, and finally embraced the technology I would need to serve others through webinars and live events, which took a lot of getting used to as presenting to a laptop camera is very different to presenting on a stage with 500 people in the audience. I wrote about the stages of change to try to help others, and was grateful for every single client I had. I set some solid small goals, one of which was to swap skills with others instead of money, so I coached a graphic designer who, in exchange, updated all my worksheets, brochures and PowerPoint slides, and I coached someone else who created free downloadable material for my site.

I turned my business around quickly and found great joy in coaching others and delivering interactive live events to corporate teams – I got the opportunity to share my skills in a new way!

Having clear, simple goals – goals to guide me, inspire me and give me a sense of achievement – was the key to the positive energy I was eventually able to create during the lockdown in Melbourne. I also employed a master life coach to push me, share the journey with me and high-five me for every small win as I fully reclaimed myself. I quickly began to flourish, to enjoy working alone again, to challenge myself and to fall back in love with the business I had created.

My health goals served me: I got so much energy from my hour-long walk on the beach every morning – I walked with a different friend every few days to keep the connections and conversations going, so we could all support each other. And though I would have found this hard to believe at first, after the first eight weeks of lockdown I was flourishing. Things became so simple with no travel, parties, dinners or social commitments. I had great boundaries around work, and I was reminded of what a gift life is. Every day I asked myself, 'What is the gift today? What is your goal today?', so I felt supported and had a clear sense of purpose.

GOAL 1	GOAL 2	GOAL 3
Why is this goal important?	Why is this goal important?	Why is this goal important?
What are three things I can do to achieve this goal?	What are three things I can do to achieve this goal?	What are three things I can do to achieve this goal?

What will it cost me if I don't follow through with these goals?

SOME GOALS TO THINK ABOUT

» Create a new online dating profile.
» Apply for that dream job.
» Take my children camping for a weekend.
» Save up to renovate part of the house.
» Host a family gathering.
» Improve my relationship with my mother-in-law.
» Spice up my marriage.
» Clear my home of clutter, old clothes and things that no longer serve me.

Write your goal of the day down every morning, and stick it where you can see it, so you have something to work towards. When you move towards your vision, it moves towards you. When you do this every day, it will move every day too.

TOP TIP - Showcase your inspiration. Hang up a quote or photo that inspires you, or program your phone to send you a positive reminder each day. Set your screensaver and wallpaper to words or images that motivate you (there are free downloadable ones at www.shannahkennedy.com). Write a reminder to yourself to be adventurous, to try something new each day. Indulge in looking at your vision board daily. All you need to do to transform your plan, to pivot with confidence, is to remind yourself to think and behave a little differently each day.

2. Write
your new
vision

1. Simplify
your life

3. Set
fresh goals

Ignite Your Flame

You have now reconnected with your powerful self. You know what you want deep down, you have a positive mindset, and have your foundational values to keep you grounded and focused. You have a vision, some large goals and smaller challenges, boundaries that give you protection and freedom, and a vision board to keep you on track. So you can now ignite the flame and get excited to take some great action.

CHOOSE YOUR CHEER SQUAD

Surround yourself with those who make you happy and want you to be happy and successful – those people who make you laugh, help you when you are in need, and genuinely care about you. They are the ones worth keeping, and everyone else can just pass through. You don't need the dream stealers or the energy zappers.

Designer Tom Ford said: 'Choose your team carefully. So much of your success is due to the people who you surround yourself with. Your friends, your family, and the people that you work with – they all play an important role in inspiring you and supporting you and giving you stability.'

These are your dream keepers, the people you want on your team to lift you higher than you ever thought possible. Enlisting the right support people is one of the best ways to boost your confidence, and this is why I work with a coach when I really want to grow, or achieve something, or need support and accountability. It is the best investment I can make. Yes, coaches need coaches. And if you have seen the Netflix series *The Last Dance*, you will know that the greatest basketball player of all time, Michael Jordan, would not have kept playing with the Chicago Bulls without the support of his coach, Phil Jackson.

We all want a life that is satisfying, purposeful and meaningful. So surround yourself with those people who lift you up, who inspire you and give you energy. You ultimately become like the people you hang out with, so do a quick stocktake of your team, and choose to spend time with loving, kind, passionate, compassionate, brilliant, energetic and giving people.

My family and true friends know that I often need to limit the amount of time I spend at social events because of my health conditions and they don't judge me for this. They support me when I feel overwhelmed or when a bout of depression begins. They get behind my goals, are my cheerleaders and carers, and give me permission to just be me. I work with a coach when I need to, a naturopath, a financial planner and an accountant. I have health and exercise friends, work friends, book club friends, schoolfriends – small groups of people who lift me up, encourage me, believe in me and are there for me when I fall down. I feel blessed to have them, but I have also made an effort to care for them as much as they care for me.

If you want to go fast, go alone. If you want to go far, go together.

African proverb

What if you treated yourself like a team? No athlete does it alone, so why should you? You can have others on your journey, be accountable to others, learn from others. Who are these go-to people?

Choose to share your new plan, your fresh pathway forward, with the right people, so they can encourage you. They will gently push you to keep going no matter what is in your way. They will support you no matter how crazy your goals may be, and they will always have your back. So who is on your team? Who are the three to five people you want with you on your journey?

1.

2.

3.

4.

5.

Who do you know who has achieved what you now dream of achieving? Meet your future peers by listing in your journal ten to twenty people you want to meet or introduce yourself to. They started where you started, were novices and dreamers once. We are all made of the same stuff.

Do a check of who gives you energy and who drains your energy. You can also find new groups to join in your area so you can connect with like-minded people with similar interests.

PRACTISE VISUALISATION

What you imagine, you create – **Anon.**

Visualise, believe, achieve. I have worked with some incredible clients, including coaches, athletes, business people and CEOs, during my time in sport and as a life strategist. I promise you that all of us have often had to accept, adapt and change our plans. Those who can visualise what they want, emotionally connect to it and believe it always achieve it. Visualisation is a form of mental rehearsal.

Once you have set your vision and goals, practise visualising yourself achieving them. This is about creating a mental picture of the desired outcome – for example, falling in love, crossing the finish line of a ten-kilometre fun run, buying that car, being happy, publishing that book, getting the job you wanted, being financially independent. See the possibility. This isn't to say that by thinking of something you will be it or have it – you still need to be prepared to work very hard for it – but visualisation is a scientifically proven performance-enhancing tool used by successful people across a range of fields. It has the power to ignite healthy emotions, in that if you practise visualising yourself reacting to challenges in a calm, gentle and compassionate way, for example, you will be more likely to manifest this behaviour.

Visualisation is not just for elite athletes – it is for everyone. No matter what stage you are at in life, visualisation is a fun and powerful way to stay positive and create the feelings and life you desire when combined with hard work, practice and a good support network. I visualise myself being light, free, happy and fun and then try to be these things as best I can. I visualise myself writing a book effortlessly, writing it with pure joy, then picture it on a shelf for someone to buy, picture it helping, supporting and guiding even just one person.

Close your eyes for five minutes and imagine your goals coming to life on a day in the near future. Imagine what you would see, hear, feel and talk about on this great day. Imagine celebrating and sharing the joy with your friends and family. Imagine the inner peace you would feel, the tingle of life giving back to you. Imagine all this as if you are already living it.

4. Be positive

3. Relax and focus

2. Use all your senses

1. Set a goal

BE THE CHANGE
YOU WISH TO SEE

Be patient when dealing with change, but start to embody it, start practising what you preach. Live towards what you wish to become – if you want love, be loving, if you want joy, be joyful, if you want confidence, believe in yourself. By simply modelling the change, you will rapidly head towards your vision and you can teach others by example.

While you cannot always rely on other people, you can direct your energy into the one thing you can count on – yourself. When we start being the change, we also lift up and inspire others, so take pride in your integrity and know that you have the strength and character to be the change you wish to see.

The green light is on. Life never stands still. Change is inevitable, it is the nature of our existence. You are not the same person you were last year or last month; you now know how to adapt, flow and roll with your plan and goals. You can enjoy the journey and know it will be smoother when you step back from grief, fear, anger and resentment and take a big breath. We can untether negative emotions and let them pass, and what seem like big problems and challenges will lose their heat and relevance over time. Your emotions will ebb and flow, but you can flow with them like the waves in the ocean.

REMEMBER, IT'S NEVER TOO LATE

To find beauty

To be free

To find a soulmate

To relax

To bounce back

To realise what's important to you

To readjust your priorities

To take control of your life

To achieve your dreams

You can be the change you wish to see . . . and you can allow Plan B to be brilliant, and also be open to plans C and D.

Let's create new memories to treasure in the future. Let's be okay with falling apart on some days and putting ourselves back together on others. Let's go from stressed to blessed with a growth mindset.

I WILL REMEMBER THAT:

- » Life doesn't happen to me, it happens for me.
- » I will nurture my resilience daily.
- » I will not let circumstances define me.
- » I can unlearn and relearn.
- » I can be the leader I would love to have.
- » I will forget perfection and instead choose progress.
- » I will let sadness pass through me.
- » I will think big, start small and begin right now.

Imagine the impact your happiness and success can have on others – how proud they will feel of you, what they will learn from your courage, and what you might inspire them to do. There are many innovative, game-changing ideas in this world, but people who actually walk the talk and bring their ideas to life, one tiny step at a time, are far rarer. I invite you to be one of these inspiring people.

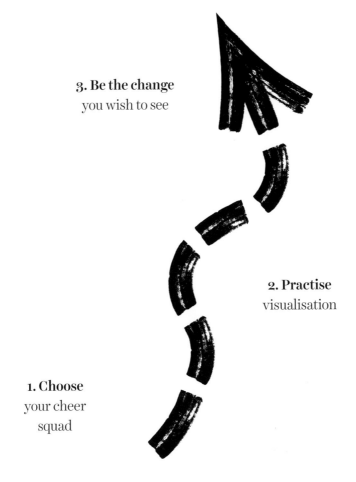

3. Be the change
you wish to see

2. Practise
visualisation

1. Choose
your cheer
squad

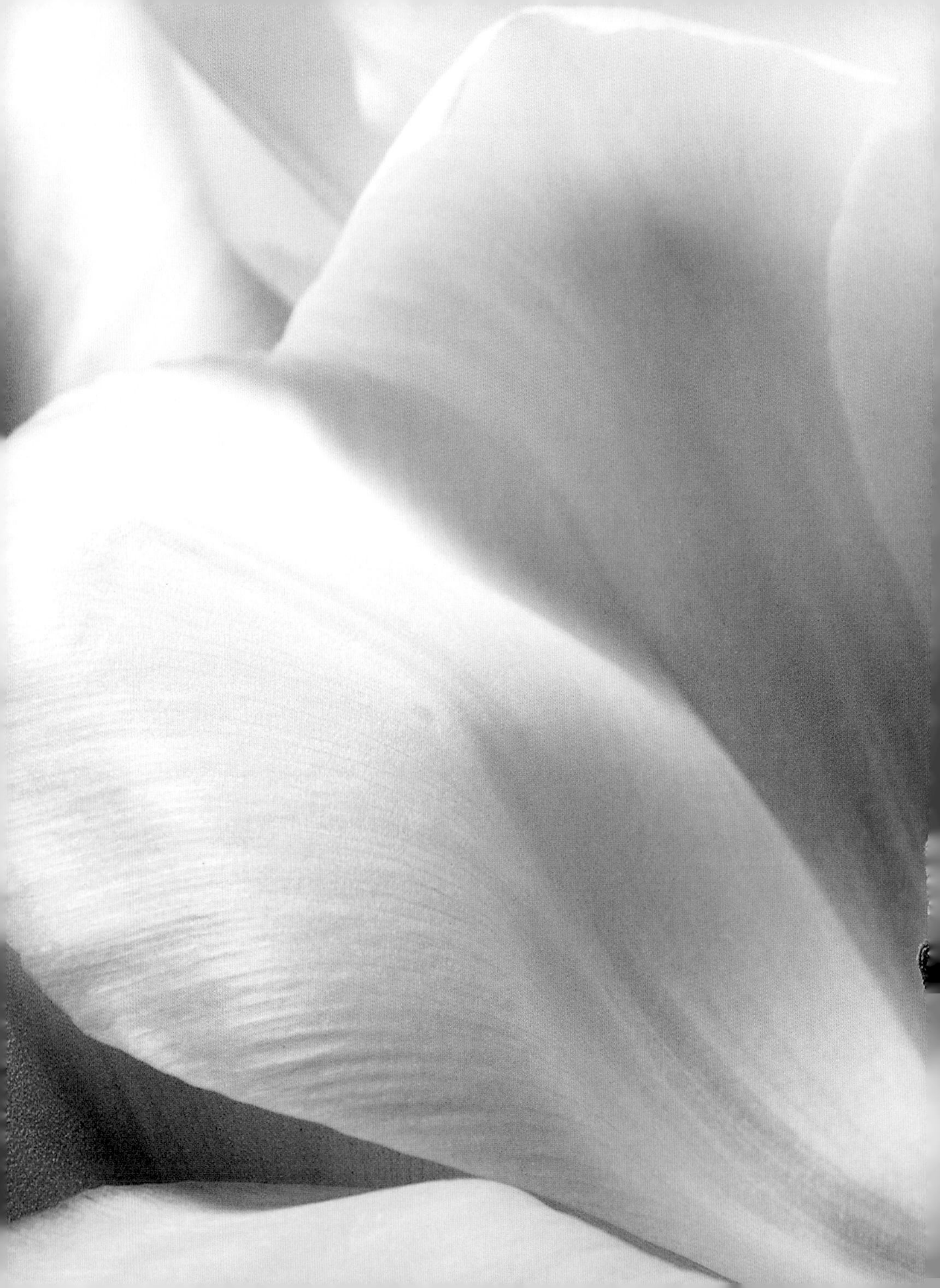

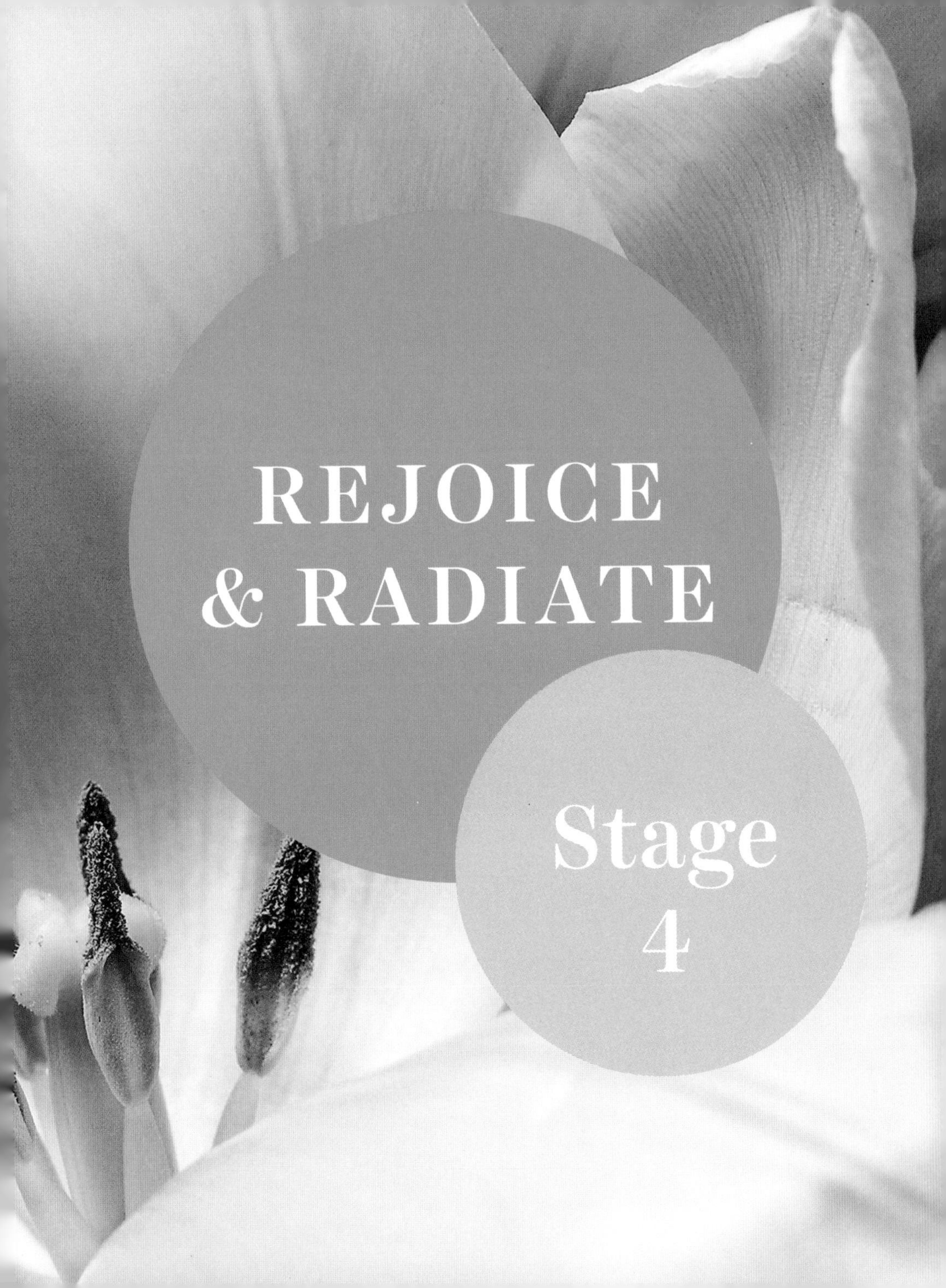

REJOICE & RADIATE

Stage 4

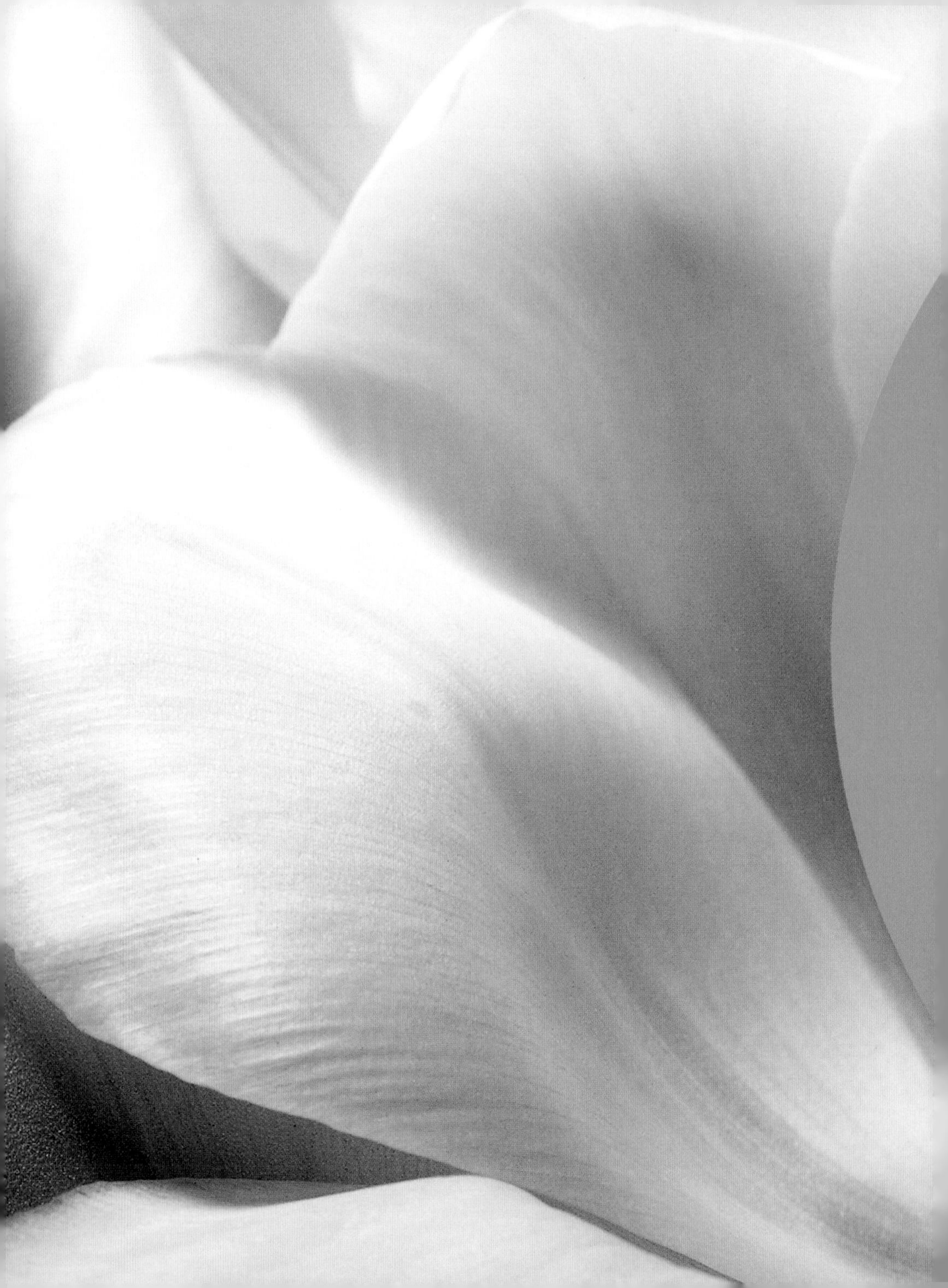

Stage 4

REJOICE & RADIATE

THE AWAKENING

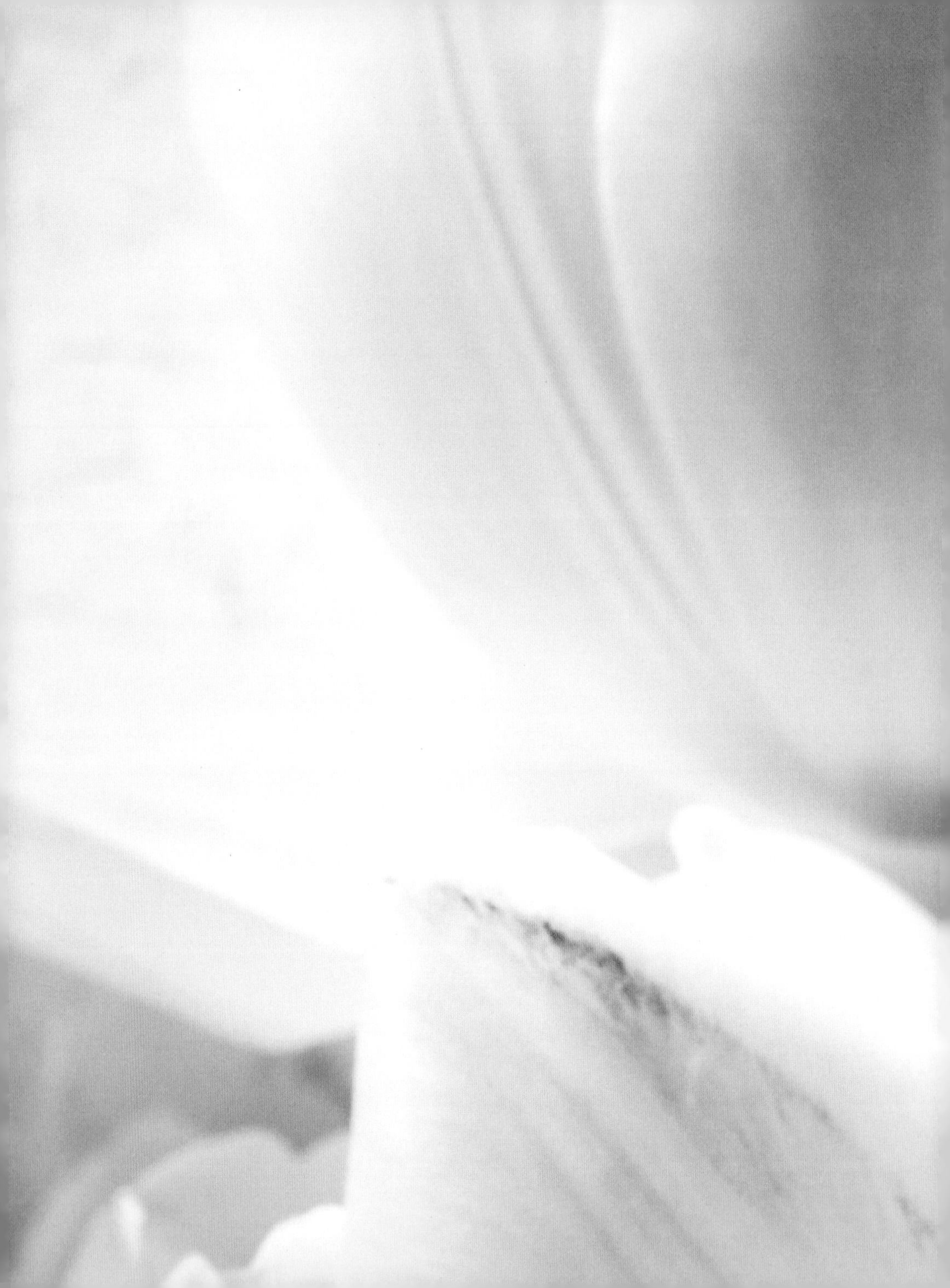

The secret
of change is to
focus all of your
energy not on
fighting the old,
but on building
the new.

This chapter is about celebrating a new era of you, sustaining and thriving in your new way of living. It will help you to truly embrace yourself and your new plans, business, relationship or life – whatever your new situation might be. It is time to love your life, to be grateful for the experiences you have been through, to marvel at how much you have grown, and to reflect on the powerful lessons you have learnt about your character and your ability to deal with change.

Now is the time to bloom once again. You may have had to alter your original plan or you may have an entirely new one. Whatever the case, the important thing is to love the vision you have set for yourself. You are more resilient now, hardier, grittier; you have shifted and experienced growth due to change, and this is your moment of awakening.

You will no doubt need to adapt to change again many times in the future, but as you put all the techniques you have learnt into practice, the pathway through change will get easier. It is a part of life. Happy people shift and persist. They understand that you just need to put one foot in front of the other, to keep your mind open to everything, to see that there really is a way forward. They accept and embrace life in all its permutations and allow it to flow on – hopefully with some magic along the way.

4. Celebrate the awakening

Experience a grateful life

Be the light

Write a letter to your future self

2. Embrace joy

Fire up your creativity

Plan your celebrations

Random acts of kindness

3. Claim your personal power

Fostering resilience and hardiness

Create your power questions

Create space for reflection

1. Embark on the journey

Manage your time and expectations

Conquer limiting beliefs

Power up your happy habits

Most people overestimate what they can do in a day and underestimate what they can do in a lifetime.

Anon

Embark on the Journey

MANAGE YOUR TIME AND EXPECTATIONS

Have you ever expected too much of yourself, or felt disappointed because your expectations were just too high? Society runs at a fast pace and it can often feel hard to keep up. It is easy to have unrealistic expectations of yourself and others, which may cause you to feel overwhelmed, anxious, exhausted, frustrated and stressed. Mindfully managing these expectations as you activate all your plans will allow you to move more easily through changes, loosen your grip and find a healthier pace, and will leave you more deeply fulfilled as you flow, flow, flow through your Plan B.

Learning to manage your expectations will allow you to plan your time wisely and set realistic goals. I have discussed these skills extensively in *The Life Plan*, and I am a great believer that mastering them will bring more joy to your life and give you a feeling of freedom.

I always advise my clients to master the basics – don't get too fancy. The way I manage my time has a direct impact on how much energy I have. I need to block out time to protect myself, to restore and recover. I need to set boundaries and they are all built into my time management. I keep a diary open on my desk and write everything in it – all my goals and commitments – and tick them off. I map out each week and create space to be human, to be my best self, by allowing myself time to practise self-care and mindfulness, which are my superpowers.

GIVE YOURSELF TIME

Healthy doses of ambition are wonderful – they fire up the soul and spark joy. I am an ambitious and driven and therefore sometimes impatient person, and it is a challenge to slow things down to take care of myself and avoid burnout. 'I give myself time' is one of my mantras, and I constantly challenge myself to pace myself, to slow the bolting horse in my mind, to find a little more balance and calmness. Be mindful of your schedule as you set daily, weekly, monthly and even yearly goals, and keep things realistic. Avoid burnout at all times.

ADAPT TO CHANGING EXPECTATIONS

As you are now fully aware, things do not always go according to plan. So when they don't work out, or take longer than expected, remember to do your breath work, reground yourself and try not to react too emotionally. Take a moment to pause, consider your options, reframe your initial expectations, respond calmly and move forward.

Top Tips

Start your day with a clear focus

Have a dynamic, prioritised task list

*Outsource and delegate what you can to free
up your time*

Make intentional compromises when needed

Minimise interruptions and distractions

Work on your most important tasks (MITs) first

Work in ninety-minute power blocks

Ask: Is it essential?

Bunch small tasks together

Learn to say no

Limit multitasking

Time-block your day

*Review your day, then celebrate and
plan the next one*

MANAGE OTHERS' EXPECTATIONS

You might have your own expectations sorted, but it can be difficult to change or manage what other people may expect of you. So be gentle and invest some time and energy into communicating with others clearly and openly.

DON'T JUDGE YOURSELF HARSHLY

Criticising yourself if you forget to do something or if you fall into a rut will get you nowhere. Judging yourself harshly for failure or when you don't live up to your goals or dreams depletes your energy and drains your confidence tank. Think of yourself as an explorer in life and remember that it's okay to learn as you go.

COMMUNICATION IS EVERYTHING

If people don't know what you need and want, how can they support you? Talk about your schedule, boundaries, likes and dislikes with others, and explain how they can support you, so they have a chance to really be there for you (and vice versa, of course).

PREPARE AGAIN

We will often face small challenges in our personal, social and working lives. That's how it goes. But I like to follow Benjamin Disraeli's ethos: 'I am prepared for the worst, but hope for the best.' I try to imagine the worst-case scenario and anticipate the many possible outcomes. This allows your mind to prepare plans C, D and E to ensure you meet your own and others' expectations even if things don't go exactly to plan.

Be aware of your expectations. Are they helpful or harmful? Learn to set a goal or intention each morning that will guide your schedule and expectations for the day.

CONQUER LIMITING BELIEFS

It is not what you say out loud that has the most power to determine your joy as you move forward, but what you whisper to yourself. Is your internal voice, your inner monologue, optimistic and full of energy, or is it limiting you with negativity? Reframing this voice is one of the biggest journeys I take people on as a coach. The only limits you have are the ones you believe.

The self-sabotaging critic in my mind needs to be trained each and every day. I am so quick now at picking up negative chatter, acknowledging it, shutting it down and replacing it with empowering thoughts.

I have coached many of my clients through the loss of a partnership, and they often say, 'How will I ever find someone again? It is going to be so hard.' And I always ask them, 'What if you allowed it to be easy and effortless? What if it is just another ride in the playground and this one is better than the last? Can you allow that?'

Your beliefs shape your every action, thought and feeling. Your reality is in many ways a reflection of your beliefs, though of course there are many other factors at play. Have a look at your life and you will see what you believe in. Consider whether you are actually lacking the things you think you are, or whether your expectations are perhaps too high. Is your mindset preventing you from having or experiencing more of these things and blocking opportunities for them to come into your life? I call this an impoverished mentality, as opposed to an abundant mentality. Having thoughts such as 'If someone else meets a life partner, that means there is less chance I will' or 'If she gets a promotion, that means I won't' suggests an impoverished mentality. Reflect on whether you might have limiting beliefs about how 'good things happen to everyone except me'.

I teach that responsibility for change rests entirely in your hands – that change happens instantly when you are committed to it, and that things must change now.

TO SHIFT FROM LIMITING TO LIMITLESS BELIEFS:

» **Acknowledge** – Can you see a pattern in your thinking? Where did it come from?

» **Trust** – That you can change and see a better way forward.

» **Replace** – Adopt a new empowering belief that brings joy, faith and energy.

LIMITING BELIEF	LIMITLESS ALTERNATIVE
I don't know how to do this	With time I can figure it out
I am not good enough	I am enough, I am constantly evolving and growing
I might fail	It's okay, failure is a part of success
It's hard to change	Change is challenging and exciting
I am too old and fixed in my ways to change	I will choose to change
I am not creative	Every human has limitless creativity
My childhood was painful	I am not a victim, I am a victor
Only very qualified people start their own businesses	Anyone can start a business
This always happens to me	A victim mentality will not serve me and I appreciate that all people need to deal with challenges
I am totally overwhelmed and can't cope	I will take three deep breaths and move forward

MY OLD LIMITING BELIEFS   **MY LIMITLESS MANTRAS**

1.

2.

3.

4.

5.

Motivation is what gets you started. Habit is what keeps you going.

Jim Ryun

POWER UP YOUR HAPPY HABITS

Habits are the small decisions you make every day. Your life is essentially the sum of your habits. How fit you feel, how happy you are and how much energy you have are largely the result of your habits. They are what you repeatedly think and do, and, as James Clear writes in *Atomic Habits*, they shape your personality and beliefs. When you power up your happy habits, you can transform your life.

Your habits determine your future. I constantly challenge, combine and tweak my habits, and I know that they are the only way I can achieve my goals and dreams while looking after myself at the same time.

Elissa, a client, came to me feeling flat – her kids had grown up and moved out and her husband was busy with his own hobbies, and she just felt quite empty. She was grieving her old life and was stuck on a treadmill, with old habits that no longer served her ruling her day. She was only fifty but she was in a rut. She had to shift, create a new plan, a fresh new inspiring road map that would give her fulfilment. We completely overhauled her habits after creating a great new vision. She identified that just having a shower before break-fast was not giving her a positive kickstart to the day or the mindset she needed to feel motivated to grow. So we set up new routines and rituals to start and finish her day that gave her energy, trained her brain, and inspired and motivated her. She got up earlier, walked for an hour, wrote in her gratitude journal, and said her affirmations in the shower. She started setting clear intentions and doing breath work, yoga and meditation. She now emails me regularly about her new hobbies, new friendships and new super amazing life. We only changed her mindset and vision for herself, and set some new goals and habits, and the effects have been enormous.

Outcomes are about what you get. Processes are about what you do. Identity is about what you believe.

James Clear

WHAT ARE THE HABITS THAT MAKE YOU HAPPY?

1.

2.

3.

4.

5.

WHAT NEW HABITS DO YOU WANT TO INTRODUCE?

1.

2.

3.

4.

5.

12 DAILY HABITS OF HAPPY PEOPLE

1 They treat themselves with kindness.

2 They let go of petty things and forgive.

3 They have tech boundaries.

4 They stay in the present.

5 They have non-negotiable rituals.

6 They keep an organised mental and physical space.

7 They allow themselves to feel emotions.

8 They put wishes into action.

9 They exercise and eat well daily.

10 They practise good decision-making.

11 They make time to recharge and be alone.

12 They smile.

Habits are structures that keep you up, keep you going and keep you happy. Take time to constantly review them, work with them and play with them so you get the results you want. Happy people build their inner world and let it radiate out to their external world. I want you to shine brightly!

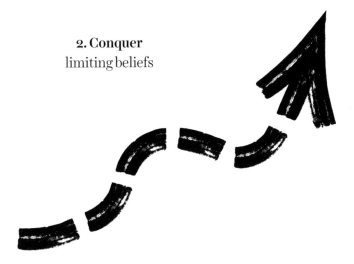

3. Power up your
happy habits

2. Conquer
limiting beliefs

1. Manage your time
and expectations

Embrace Joy

FIRE UP YOUR CREATIVITY

As Elizabeth Gilbert says in *Big Magic*, 'A creative life is an amplified life . . . a bigger life, a happier life, an expanded life, and a hell of a lot more interesting life . . . creative living is a path for the brave.' I like to think that fear is boring, and that when my courage dies, my creativity dies with it. Just like an incredibly toned athlete who can spring into action immediately, those who consciously and regularly access their core creativity become creatively toned. And when you are creatively toned, you don't just dip your toe in the water and stay safe, you jump in and are utterly daring and fight off your limiting beliefs with a 'Yes I can!'

I can tell you that when you sit down to write the very first word of a book, fear grips you. What if the words don't flow out? What if it just doesn't work? But you can switch to courage and place one word after another, and just try, because the less you fight fear, the less it fights back. Just stay with the process and don't panic. Remind yourself: 'I am writing regardless of the result. I am writing this because I truly believe there is a place for this book in the world right now, so I am going to make it happen.' Gilbert encourages us to let curiosity rather than fear drive us, because our inner creativity is waiting to come out. She says: 'Creativity is a crushing chore and a glorious mystery. The work wants to be made, and it wants to be made through you.' I see myself as solely responsible for producing the work, and I agree with Gilbert's assertion that if you can just complete something you are miles ahead of the pack.

So I invite you to find your life, your work and your relationships a source of love and creative joy. Do not dabble too much in drama and remember that a burst of inspiration is always nearby.

CURIOSITY IS THE PATH TO CREATIVITY. TO START THE FLAME OF CREATIVITY, ASK YOURSELF THESE QUESTIONS ALL THE TIME

What am I curious about? What do I find interesting today?

No matter how mundane or small this thing is, it is your seed.

ACTIVITIES TO SPARK YOUR CREATIVITY

» Creative writing

» Journalling

» Essential oils

» Growing herbs

» Coastal walks

» Understanding more about the food you are eating

» Flower arranging

» Different breathing techniques

» Learning how to grow vegetables

» Researching your family tree

» Knitting

» Painting

» Jewellery design

» Dance

» Poetry

» Understanding different yoga poses

» Learning how to best invest your money

» Giving back

» Volunteering

I AM INTERESTED IN OR CURIOUS ABOUT:

1.

2.

3.

4.

5.

6.

What would you do even if you knew you might fail?
It is in creativity that you will grow.

The more you praise and celebrate your life, the more there is in life to celebrate.

Oprah Winfrey

PLAN YOUR CELEBRATIONS

Toss some confetti in the air! How will you celebrate both your small wins and your bigger goals? I often observe people going from one goal to the next without a pause in between to honour their commitment and sit in joy for a minute. When your new plan is in action, be there, pay attention and embrace some serious high-fives! Celebrating is contagious, it creates momentum and it is a well-deserved reward for all the work you have done. So do your dance, turn up the music, pop the champagne, have some fun, let your hair down, jump up and down – I give you permission!

WAYS TO CELEBRATE

» **Send a thankyou card or gift to the people who supported you** – Who will you send them to? What will you send?

» **Purchase something special** – What will you get? What will you do with it?

» **Take a trip** – Where will you go? What will you do there?

» **Book some time out** – What will you do? How will you restore?

» **Book a special dinner** – Where will you go? Who will you invite?

» **Throw a party** – Who will you invite? What will you say as a toast?

MY CELEBRATIONS

Small wins:

....

....

....

....

Big wins:

....

....

....

....

Top Tip

*Create a visual reminder of
your plan to inspire yourself:
a picture of the trip or the special
purchase or the restaurant you
are going to. When the celebrations
have wrapped up, how will you
help others to achieve
what you have?*

I celebrate every day. Each day in my journal I answer the question: 'What three amazing things happened today?' Even on days when I feel flat or have no energy, I can think of three amazing things that happened.

THREE AMAZING THINGS THAT HAPPENED TODAY:

1.

2.

3.

Don't forget to celebrate yourself! You will love completing this list
and looking back at it. Celebrate your achievements, strength and
character, and all that you are doing. Put in a couple of future 'rocks'
also, for things you are planning to do.

I rock because

I rock because

I rock because

I rock because

I rock because

My religion is
very simple.
My religion is
kindness.

_____

Dalai Lama

RANDOM ACTS OF KINDNESS

As Aesop said, 'No act of kindness, no matter how small, is ever wasted.' You can be the reason someone smiles today. When you perform random acts of kindness you release positivity. You and the recipient feel better, which will help them to be kind to others too. It is about spreading love and joy.

Whether through a smile, making someone laugh or volunteering your help, look for opportunities throughout your day to show those around you – people you know or complete strangers – that they are worthy and valued.

Every night at the dinner table we talk about the rose and the thorn of our day, and what random acts of kindness we have performed. This is a simple dinner ritual that connects us as a family, fills our cup of happiness and reminds us to stay on the kindness path.

RANDOM ACTS OF KINDNESS	Pay for someone's coffee.	Say 'good morning' to the person next to you.
Say 'I love you' to someone.	Let someone into your lane when driving.	Ask someone: 'How are you really doing?'
Smile when crossing paths with a stranger.	Call a friend.	Give someone a hug.
Bring your partner breakfast in bed.	Take 15 minutes to listen to someone.	Help someone try something new.
Share your favourite recipe.	Talk to someone who is shy.	Post some nice comments on social media.
Give up your seat on the bus or train.	Reconnect with an old friend.	Do someone a favour.
Thank a teacher with a gift.	Bake a cake for someone.	Take the neighbour's dog for a walk.
Run an errand for someone.	Mow your neighbour's lawn.	Send flowers for no reason.
Hold the door open for someone.	Pick up rubbish that isn't yours.	Leave a tip.
Leave someone a nice note.	Text a friend a happy face.	Give someone a compliment.

MY FAVOURITE RANDOM ACTS OF KINDNESS ARE:

....

....

....

....

....

As well as giving, remember to be open to receiving.

No one will talk about how much money you have, how many deals you did, how many goals you kicked, or how many medals or awards you won. They will remember how you made them feel, and you cannot give what you have not cultivated in yourself.

3. Random acts
of kindness

1. Fire up your
creativity

2. Plan your
celebrations

The species
that survives is the
one that is able best
to adapt and adjust
to the changing
environment in
which it finds itself.

Leon C.
Megginson

Claim Your Personal Power

FOSTERING RESILIENCE AND HARDINESS

Resilience can be defined as the capacity to recover quickly from difficulties. You cannot prevent change or adversity, but you can work with them to become hardier, more resilient. It is well worth taking a bit of time to understand how resilience is built so you can be mindful of it as you deal with challenges, reclaim your personal power and journey towards self-mastery.

Dr Ken Ginsburg, child paediatrician and human-development expert, proposes that there are seven interrelated components integral to resilience – competence, confidence, connection, character, contribution, coping and control. These components invite us to find strength amid uncertainty.

The American Psychological Association has a list of ten ways you can foster resilience and hardiness. This is my go-to list. When you feel like you need a pick-me-up and want to remind yourself of how to strengthen your resilience muscle, see what actions you can take from this list.

1   Make connections. Accepting help and support from those who care about you and will listen to you strengthens resilience.

2   Avoid seeing crises as insurmountable problems. Try looking beyond the present to how future circumstances may be a little better.

3   Accept that change is a part of living. Accepting circumstances that cannot be changed can help you focus on circumstances you can alter.

4   Move towards your goals. Do something regularly – even if it seems like a small accomplishment – that enables you to move towards your goals.

5   Take decisive action. Rather than detaching completely from problems and stresses and wishing they would just go away, act on adverse situations as much as you can.

6   Look for opportunities for self-discovery. People often learn something about themselves through their struggle with loss and may find that they have grown in some respect.

7   Nurture a positive view of yourself. Developing confidence in your ability to solve problems and trusting your instincts helps build resilience.

8   Keep things in perspective. Even when facing very painful events, try to consider the stressful situation in a broader context and keep a long-term perspective.

9   Maintain a hopeful outlook. Try visualising what you want, rather than worrying about what you fear.

10 Take care of yourself. Pay attention to your own needs and feelings. Engage in activities that you enjoy and find relaxing.

Being resilient doesn't mean being happy all the time. Negative emotions such as loneliness, envy, guilt, fear and anger all have an important role to play in your happy life. They are simply white flags being raised to tell you something needs to change.

CREATE YOUR
POWER QUESTIONS

Knowledge is power and intelligence is asking the right questions. Coaches ask questions. We ask them and we listen and then we turn the light on for the client. I have questions on my wall to spark my curiosity and as a constant reminder to keep reflecting and reconnecting with myself (as self-connection is at the heart of a happy and successful life), find my resilience and build great habits. These questions are short and powerful and instantly bring you home to yourself.

MY FAVOURITE DAILY QUESTIONS

'What is my goal of the day?' This gives me clarity, focus and purpose.

'What would love do?' This softens me and takes the edge off my big emotions.

'What am I grateful for?' This allows me to lean in to change and to problems that arise, and gives me a healthier mindset.

I invite you to develop your own morning and evening questions for your journal. Here is a list you can start from.

MORNING QUESTIONS

What is most important to me right now?

What am I grateful for?

What would make today great?

What is my affirmation for the day?

What am I happy about in this moment?

What do I feel excited about?

What do I really want?

What can I let go of today?

How can I be kind today?

What am I proud of right now?

Who do I love right now?

Who cares for me right now?

What am I going to create today?

What am I going to try today?

What would love do?

What is procrastination costing me?

EVENING QUESTIONS

What three amazing things happened today?

How could I have made today even better?

What did I learn today?

What did I give today?

What is my wiser self telling me to do tomorrow?

What is most important to me right now?

MY THREE MORNING POWER QUESTIONS

1.

....

2.

....

3.

....

MY THREE EVENING POWER QUESTIONS

1.

....

2.

....

3.

....

....

You will feel great when you take the time to write in your journal and answer questions that always bring you back to yourself. For every question, search for three answers.

Time spent in self-reflection is never wasted – it is an intimate date with yourself.

Dr Paul T. P. Wong

CREATE SPACE FOR REFLECTION

Remember that clarity, wisdom, peace and success all come from within. Amid the hustle, be aware of the healing powers of reflection and stillness, stopping and creating some space so you can catch your breath, avoid burnout and bathe in the journey of your life.

Reflection is about careful thought. You can do it anywhere, alone or with anyone, and it can even take the form of writing or having a conversation. It is about allowing yourself to consciously reflect on your memories, how far you have come, and what is and isn't working for you at the moment.

Reflection is best when scheduled, perhaps on one of those precious weekend mornings where you can dedicate an hour to yourself. I like to sit in a coffee shop to pause, think and write and process everything that is happening. I like to walk the dog on my own and reflect, slow my mind down, simply be human again. To remember that life is not a race, to stop and smell the roses . . . if these are things you are avoiding, this is something to reflect on. Great athletes, great leaders and successful people of all kinds make time to reflect, as it is by reflecting that they can truly see.

Noticing and creating moments of stillness each and every day is pure bliss, and can inject an enormous amount of clarity, energy and fulfilment into your life. So get great at finding snippets of stillness, pockets of silence, and mindfully and intentionally taking them.

Those moments when the house is totally quiet, or when you are washing your hands in the bathroom, or putting the washing on, can be moments of stillness. Whether you are at a traffic light, on public transport or standing in a queue, you have the opportunity to tap into stillness, to wake up and notice how you are feeling, so press pause and soak in the luxurious calm. When you park your car, take three slow breaths, or before you drive off again, sit still and take six deep belly breaths. Be attentive wherever you can – take a short pause before sending an email, or simply touch a tree when in nature instead of walking past it. You may even want to notice the incredible momentary pause between your inhale and exhale, the spaces between your thoughts. Just slow it all down and find the mini moments. When you give time to quiet experience, you change your vibration, and when you change your vibration you change your world.

As I've mentioned, my promise to myself is to be still, reflect and meditate for twenty minutes every afternoon. It is so empowering to just stop and take a breath, to just be, here, now.

When I work with clients, I often ask them to pause, to take a breath, to sit and acknowledge where they have come from. It is in this moment that tears of joy are often shed, that they tap into an incredible feeling of fulfilment, self-appreciation and self-love. I often allow myself these moments now too. I never used to, as I thought they were a waste of time and overly indulgent, but now I see them as a superpower. This is where joy sits: clarity comes and I feel deeply grounded. Why aren't we taught this at school? I've noticed that clients are good at reflecting on what isn't working for them, they ruminate on it, over-analyse it, sit in the stench of it, are paralysed by it. But when they learn to reflect on what is going well – what is working, what opportunities exist around them – they tap into their sense of freedom and realise that everything we do is a choice. How we think, how we react, how we spend our time – this is all a choice.

Make reflection, stillness and mindfulness a part of the joy in your life. Seek them out in small moments, but also schedule some time in your diary for yourself. I often ask my clients to book a date with themselves, to just sit in a café or go for a walk, to ponder and fully inhabit themselves, as that is the way to clarity.

I like to use the analogy of filling up a glass from the river. At first the water is murky and swirling. But when you sit the glass down and invite stillness, the sediment slowly falls to the bottom, the water becomes translucent and clarity presents itself. Give yourself the gift of clarity, the most powerful gift of all.

I WILL FIND MOMENTS OF CLARITY AND STILLNESS BY:

1.

2.

3.

4.

You need to mindfully and willingly invite reflection and stillness – they will not automatically appear in your busy life. They are your power tools and your pathway to self-mastery, self-management and self-leadership.

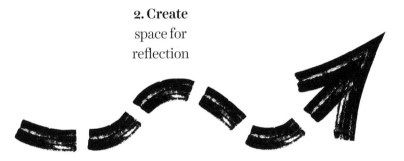

3. Resilience
and hardiness

2. Create
space for
reflection

1. Create
your power
questions

A grateful heart is a magnet for miracles.

Anon

Celebrate the Awakening

EXPERIENCE A GRATEFUL LIFE

I am truly grateful and blessed for twenty years of incredible life experiences with clients, for every conversation, every cup of coffee, every stage I spoke on, every bookstore I signed books in, and every scary and challenging moment my career has thrown at me. I have been scared like no tomorrow before walking onto a stage before a packed audience, had butterflies, sleepless nights, 4 am starts for early flights, sheer exhaustion from some massive days that nearly tipped me over. But I am truly thankful for all these things as they have taken me to where I am today.

I am grateful for every book I have read, every podcast I have listened to and every TED talk I have watched. Even when I didn't enjoy them, I still learnt something. I am grateful for all the rejections and the jobs I didn't get, because at the end of the day they were not meant to be mine. I am grateful for everyone who has believed in me and supported me.

I am grateful for the family members, friends, coaches, role models, doctors, naturopaths, social media followers and others who support and have supported me, who hold up a mirror for me and remind me to slow things down, to enjoy the journey, to just care, really care, for myself and all the people in my life.

It took me a long time and quite a lot of practice to truly embrace this way of life. Not to just write about gratitude or think about it occasionally or give it lip service, but to truly embody it. I invite you now to do the same. I write it daily, I think it often, but I feel it in my bones. I believe that even days when I don't feel well or feel totally paralysed are days sent to speak to me. To remind me to care for myself and others.

I AM MOST GRATEFUL FOR:

1.

2.

3.

4.

5.

6.

7.

Be grateful to yourself as you go on this journey of self-empowerment.

Be the light that helps others see.

Roy T. Bennett

BE THE LIGHT

No matter what you have been through, you can move on and be a light for others. Can you allow yourself to shine brightly and fully embrace your Plan B?

My clients often refer to me as their lighthouse. I want to be a light for others if I can, by sharing my stories, my life and my way of thinking. They may not suit everyone, but if they help another person I am happy. I often challenge myself to be a light for my family and friends, and I trust that the universe will guide me.

So allow yourself to shine brightly, to be truly happy again, to be a source of light for others.

WRITE A LETTER TO YOUR FUTURE SELF

What have you learnt from accepting, adapting, restoring and recreating yourself on this journey? What do you want to say to your future self? Writing a letter to your future self is a beautiful act of kindness and self-care. You will face many storms in life, and hopefully they are all relatively small, but if you have a heartfelt letter reminding you of what you have learnt and promised yourself, you will always have comfort. So take time to write this letter to yourself and record your most important lessons in it.

LESSONS TO GUIDE YOU AS YOU MOVE FORWARD

» **Pace yourself** – Let life unfold a little.

» **Happiness is not for sale** – Money can't buy happiness.

» **You can't please everyone** – Beware of the disease to please.

» **Don't hesitate when you should act** – Seize the day.

» **Good things don't come easy** – There is no reward without effort.

» **Never fail to try again** – You might not get it right the first time, and that's okay.

» **Take care of your health early on** – It is your most valuable asset.

» **Don't let your tank get empty** – Top it up with acts of self-care.

» **You don't always get what you want** – Even the best plans can go awry.

» **Make every moment count** – Life moves quickly.

» **Love is more than a feeling** – It is a choice you make every day.

» **Perspective is a beautiful thing** – It makes problems and challenges seem smaller.

» **Live and let live** – Don't force your ideas onto someone else.

» **Be flexible with your goals** – Faster isn't always better.

» **You are enough as you are** – Don't compare yourself with others.

3. Write a letter to your future self

2. Be the light

1. Experience a grateful life

ONE LAST THING

Everyone experiences change, to differing degrees. But at some point, consciously or not, we will all go through the four stages described in this book. Whether we are dealing with work or financial insecurity, a broken relationship, a change in living circumstances, a serious illness or the loss of a loved one, we will go through a process of acceptance, healing, reorienting and eventually moving forward.

I hope this book has helped you to understand the path that life will take you on when you are faced with change and need to accept, adapt and create a new plan. Know that this book can be your guide for the rest of your life. You can turn to it for encouragement, motivation and advice as you grapple with changes and challenges, no matter how big or small, and learn to move past them.

Plan B can be full of hidden gifts, treasures and incredible experiences, as can plans C and D. Knowing how to shift your mindset, restore yourself and adapt your strategies, habits, routines, rituals and thought processes to your new situation will be your hidden superpower.

May you shine bright, no matter where you are in life, and know that you are not alone. Be strong and be gentle with yourself and others – you've got this.

With much warmth and gratitude,

Shannah Kennedy

THANK YOU

To all the role models and teachers out there who have taught me how to navigate change both personally and professionally.

To each and every client I have worked with during my twenty years of coaching, for trusting me, sharing a part of your life with me and allowing me to be your lighthouse.

To my husband, Michael, you are my forever number one, you always believe in me and my ideas and cheer me on. And to my teenage children Jack and Mia, who challenge me each and every day to be the best version of myself. You are my world.

To my mum and dad, who between them have been through divorce, accidents, health crisis after health crisis, the loss of a parent at a very early age, and the loss of jobs – who have endured some deeply disappointing times and still been the light for all of us. You have taught me, my brother and my sister to keep life simple, stay grounded and focus on the basics as a foundation for happiness.

To the amazing team at Penguin Random House, who listen to my ideas, believe in me and support the new ideas and visions I bring to them. I thank you for the time and effort you put into my books.

To my extended family and friends, and my coach through a year of COVID-19, thanks for never being dream stealers. I appreciate wholeheartedly your encouragement as I 'just go for it' and say 'yes' to my goals, as I take massive action and try to quieten my inner critic.

Finally, to you, the reader – it is because of you I write these books. To all those who purchased *The Life Plan: Simple strategies for a meaningful life* and shared with me stories of how the book changed your life. You gave me the courage to keep writing and I am ever grateful that you took the time to write to me; you brightened my days and topped up my level of fulfilment in life. Thank you for the privilege of writing for you. I would love to hear from you and learn how *Plan B* supported you through change. I hope this book gave you a hug, inspired you and showed you how to navigate and embrace change to shine brightly once again.

ABOUT
THE AUTHOR

Shannah Kennedy is one of Australia's foremost strategic life coaches. She works to transform her clients' careers, wellbeing and lives. She specialises in executive strategy, transition, values, vision, overcoming burnout and life planning for individuals. Her proven expertise enables clients to gain control of their lives in order to achieve their visions and goals and find happiness and fulfilment.

She is the bestselling author of *The Life Plan*, a wellbeing specialist, keynote speaker, workshop facilitator and media contributor, and a wife and mother of two. Shannah lives and dances with chronic fatigue syndrome and depression and is committed to living her best and most energetic life based on her values and commitment to authenticity.

Shannah is a master of simplicity and presents the most powerful and essential life and wellness skill sets to transform the way you live and work, create clarity, direction and purpose, and shine a light on the benefits of self-care, self-management and self-leadership.

Visit **www.shannahkennedy.com** for further information, free resources and to get in touch.

PENGUIN LIFE

UK | USA | Canada | Ireland | Australia
India | New Zealand | South Africa | China

Penguin Life is part of the Penguin Random House group of companies whose
addresses can be found at global.penguinrandomhouse.com

First published by Penguin Life in 2021

Cover and internal design and infographics (except for Feeling Wheel on page 36)
by Louisa Maggio © Penguin Random House Australia Pty Ltd
Photography by Sharyn Cairns
Author photograph by Rachel Devine
Typeset in Harriet by Louisa Maggio © Penguin Random House Australia Pty Ltd

Printed and bound in Singapore

 A catalogue record for this
book is available from the
National Library of Australia

ISBN 978 1 76104 107 5

penguin.com.au